Introduction

The motorcycle. An iron horse, ridden by today's adventurer in the same fashion that the cowboy traveled in America's old west. Just my ride and me. The feeling I've had as I've crossed the Great Plains or cruised north inside the Wyoming border feeling like the landscape is that of a Road Runner cartoon is that my whole world is contained on my machine. My possessions, my mode of transport, all powered by an engine situated between two wheels and fed by a flow of fuel from the tank sitting between my legs. Saddlebags are holding my stuff. Shelter and clothing strapped on a rack, held in place by a cargo net or bungee chords. Sometimes I travel with a friend who rides his cycle. Sometimes with a new girl on the back holding on to me. Other times…alone. It all fits into the mystique of the road. Me vs. the world and things can sometimes go wrong. The engine sputters and I find out it's in need of a new fuel filter, which I replace for under two bucks in the next town, or the bike dies and I find out that I'm out of gas and should have switched to reserve. A tire blows and I'm a thousand miles from home pushing the bike down the shoulder of a state highway in the middle of nowheresville, Kansas.

Motorcyclists vary with their desires. Some like speed. Some like the open road. We're law-abiding travelers with a flair for adventure that involves climbing up a few rungs on the ladder of risk. I ride through the rain, or in one hundred degree heat. With a helmet, without a helmet, depending on the laws of the state I'm passing through, I rent a campsite at the end of the day and untie my tent and sleeping bag from the luggage rack, build a fire, cook up some grub and drink my beverage of choice for the night. Maybe smoke a cigar…or something else.

Some motorcyclists don't even leave their town. One hundred miles is the longest trip they've ever taken, not three thousand. No, there is no formula or reasoning for a person who sets out for adventure on a motorcycle, but there are unwritten codes. Keep the rubber side down, don't go over the high side, or "You're gonna' be my bitch on the back this trip", to name a few. No matter what the view, so far what I'm telling falls under the jurisdiction of what the American Motorcyclist Association calls the ninety nine percent of the motorcyclist population. The law-abiding citizens. The rest are known as the one percenters. That is what this book is about. We'll begin with the Hollister riot that started the stereotype of the "Outlaw Motorcyclist."

-A.W. Ellison

The Hollister Incident

The **Hollister Incident** was an event that occurred at the American Motorcyclist Association (AMA) sanctioned Gypsy Tour motorcycle rally in Hollister, California from July 3-6, 1947.

Many more motorcyclists than expected flooded the small town to watch the annual rallies as well as to socialize and drink. A very few of the motorcyclists got out of control and caused a commotion in the town, although at the end of the event, the damage was considered minor.

The small incident, known afterwards as the Hollister riot, was sensationalized by the press with reports of bikers "taking over the town" and "pandemonium" in Hollister. The strongest dramatization of the event was a staged photo of a drunken man sitting on a motorcycle surrounded by beer bottles. It was published in *Life* magazine and it brought national attention and negative opinion to the event. The Hollister riot helped to give rise to the outlaw biker image.

Rise of motorcycles after World War II

After World War II, countless veterans came back to America and many of them had a difficult time readjusting to civilian life. They searched for the adventure and adrenaline rush associated with life at war that had now left them. Civilian life felt too monotonous for some men who also craved feelings of excitement and danger. Others sought the close bonds and camaraderie found between men in the army. Furthermore, certain men wanted to combat their horrifying war memories and experiences that haunted them, many in the form of Post Traumatic Stress Disorder. Thus, motorcycling emerged stronger than ever as a substitute for wartime experiences such as adventure, excitement, danger and camaraderie. Men who had been a part of the motorcycling world before the war were now joined by thousands of new members. The popularity of motorcycling grew dramatically after World War II because of the effects of the war on veterans.

Event

Throughout the 1930s, Hollister, California hosted an annual Fourth of July gypsy tour event. Gypsy tours were American Motorcyclist Association sanctioned racing events that took place all over America and were considered to be the best place for motorcyclists to converge. The annual event consisted of motorcycle races, social activities, and lots of partying. In Hollister, the event and the motorcyclists were very welcome. Especially because Hollister was a very small town, with only about 4,500 people, the rally became a major event in its yearly life as well as an important part of the town's economy. Due to World War II, the rally was canceled, but the event organized for 1947 was the revival of the Gypsy Tour in Hollister.

On July 3, 1947, the festivities in Hollister began. But as previously mentioned, the popularity of motorcycles grew dramatically and this rise in popularity caused one of the main problems of this event: massive attendance. Around 4,000 motorcyclists flooded Hollister, almost doubling the population of the small town. They came from all over California and the United States, even from as far away as Connecticut and Florida. Motorcycle groups in attendance included the Pissed Off Bastards of Bloomington, the Boozefighters, the Market Street Commandos and the Galloping Goose Motorcycle Club. Approximately ten percent of attendees were women. The town was completely unprepared for the number of people that arrived. The large attendance was unexpected since not nearly as many people had come in previous years.

Initially, the motorcyclists were welcomed into the Hollister bars, as the influx of people was great for business. But soon, they started causing a problem in Hollister. The drunken motorcyclists were riding their bikes through the small streets of Hollister and consuming huge amounts of alcohol. They were fighting, damaging bars, throwing beer bottles out of windows, racing in the streets, and other drunken actions. Also, there was a severe housing problem. The bikers had to sleep on sidewalks, in parks, in haystacks and on people's lawns. By the evening of July 4th, "they were virtually out of control".

This was all too much for the seven-man police force of Hollister to handle. The police tried to stop the motorcyclists' activities by threatening to use tear gas and by arresting as many drunken men as they could. Also, the bars tried in vain to stop the men from drinking by refusing to sell beer and voluntarily closing two hours ahead of time.

Eyewitnesses were quoted as saying, "It's just one hell of a mess", but that "[the motorcyclists] weren't doing anything bad, just riding up and down whooping and hollering; not really doing any harm at all."

The ruckus continued through July 5th and slowly died out at the end of the weekend as the rallies ended and the motorcyclists left town.

At the end of the Fourth of July weekend and the informal riot, Hollister was littered with thousands of beer bottles and other debris and there was some minor storefront damage. About 50 people were arrested, most with misdemeanors such as public intoxication, reckless driving, and disturbing the peace. There were around 60 reported injuries, of which 3 were serious, including a broken leg and skull fracture. Other than having to witness the chaos of the weekend, no Hollister residents suffered any harm at all. A City-Council member stated, "Luckily, there appears to be no serious damage. These trick riders did more harm to themselves than the town."

Media coverage

The small riot came to national prominence through media coverage of the event. However, the articles that were written about the riot were greatly exaggerated and sensationalized the actual events.

Firstly, shortly after the Fourth of July weekend, two articles were published in the San Francisco Chronicle. With titles "Havoc in Hollister" and "Hollister's Bad Time", they both described the event as "pandemonium" and "terrorism". While the articles did not actually lie about the events that occurred, the perspectives of the articles were both negative toward the motorcyclists involved. The Chronicle article did little to cause panic for citizens in the California area as there was other major news occurring at the same time, including local labor strikes. Yet, the press reports of the Hollister riot did expand past California with an article published in the July 21, 1947 issue of Life Magazine. Life Magazine was a major American publication and this brought the riot to national prominence. The article was published in the section of

Life that relied heavily on graphic images and sparse explanatory text. This was shown as the article included only a nearly full-page photo, a small 115-word insert of text at the bottom of the page and the headline, "Cyclist's Holiday: He and Friends Terrorize Town."

Eddie Davenport of Tulare, California on a motorcycle, with August 'Gus' Deserpa standing behind, in Hollister on July 7, 1947, by the *San Francisco Chronicle*'s photographer Barney Petersen.

Date: July 4, 1947–July 6, 1947
Location: Hollister, California
Also known as: 1947 Hollister Gypsy Tour
Participants: 2,000 to 4,000 attendees, including about 750 motorcyclists. Members of the American Motorcyclist Association, Boozefighters, Pissed Off Bastards of Bloomington and other motorcycle clubs

The large photo, taken by Barney Peterson of the *San Francisco Chronicle*, shows a drunken man, sitting atop a Harley-Davidson motorcycle, holding a beer bottle in each hand and surrounded by many other empty, broken bottles. The man was later identified as Eddie Davenport, a member of the Tulare Riders motorcycle club.

However, the reliability of the striking photo has been debated, as many sources say that it was staged. The photograph was taken by Barney Petersen of the *San Francisco Chronicle*. The Chronicle did not run any images of the event. Many eyewitnesses argue that the image was staged. For example, Gus Deserpa is the man that can be seen in the background of the photograph. When he was interviewed after the Hollister riot, he said, "I saw two guys scraping all these bottles together, that had been lying in the street. Then they positioned a motorcycle in the middle of the pile. After a while this drunk guy comes staggering out of the bar, and they got him to sit on the motorcycle, and started to take his picture."

Barney Peterson's colleague at the *Chronicle*, photographer Jerry Telfer, said it was implausible that Peterson would have faked the photos. Telfer said, "Barney was not the type to fake a picture. Barney was the kind of fellow who had a very keen sense of ethics, pictorial ethics as well as word ethics."

Consequences

The news of rogue motorcyclists causing havoc in small towns such as Hollister was not comforting to Americans still recovering from World War II and scared about the impending Cold War. The nation started to fear motorcycle "hoodlums" and potential rampages.

The AMA released a statement saying that they had no involvement with the Hollister riot, and, "the trouble was caused by the one per cent deviant that tarnishes the public image of both motorcycles and motorcyclists" and that the other ninety-nine per cent of motorcyclists are good, decent, law-abiding citizens. However, the American Motorcyclist Association has no record of ever releasing such a statement. A representative of the AMA said in 2005, "we've been unable to attribute [the term 'one-percenter] original use to an AMA official or published statement — so it's apocryphal." The AMA's statement led to one-percenter being widely used to describe outlaw motorcycle clubs and motorcyclists.

The Hollister riot had little effect on the town itself. The nationwide fear of motorcyclists did not result in many changes in Hollister. Bikers were welcomed back and rallies continued to be held in the years after the riot. In fact, the town held a 1997 50th anniversary rally to commemorate the event.

Adaptations

A short story, *Cyclists' Raid*, by Frank Rooney is based on the events of the Hollister riot and was originally published in the January 1951 issue of Harper's Magazine. This story made up the basis of the plot of the 1953 film *The Wild One*, starring Marlon Brando. However, as a dramatized version, it bears little resemblance to the actual events of the Hollister riot. The movie only worked to further bring the riot into public light and with motorcyclists portrayed as misfits and outlaws, it eliminated any way to salvage motorcycling's already tarnished image

Here are the "One Percenter" Outlaw Motorcycle Clubs of Earth, as found in **Wikipedia, the free online encyclopedia.**

Bandidos Motorcycle Club

Bandidos Motorcycle Club

Motto: We are the people our parents warned us about
Founded: 1966
Location: San Leon, Texas
Founder: Donald Eugene Chambers
Type: Outlaw motorcycle club

Region: Worldwide
Website: www.bandidosmc.com

The **Bandidos Motorcycle Club**, also known as the **Bandido Nation**, is a "one-percenter" motorcycle gang and organized crime syndicate with a worldwide membership. The club was formed in 1966 by Don Chambers in Texas. Its motto is "We are the people our parents warned us about". It is estimated to have 2,400 members in 210 chapters, located in 22 countries. The club considers itself to be an outlaw motorcycle club. The Federal Bureau of Investigation and the Criminal Intelligence Service Canada have named the Bandidos an "outlaw motorcycle gang".

Organization

The Bandidos has over 90 chapters in the United States, 90 chapters in Europe, and another 17 in Australia, 1 in New Zealand and In Southeast Asia.

In North America

In the United States, the club is concentrated in Texas, but extends into Louisiana, Mississippi, Alabama, Arkansas, New Mexico, Colorado, Montana, Wyoming, South Dakota, Utah, Idaho, Nevada, Washington, Oklahoma, Nebraska, and several other states.

In Canada, the Rock Machine Motorcycle club in Montréal merged with the Bandidos in 2000; there was a chapter in Toronto, Ontario until a dramatic internal conflict led to their deaths.

In Oceania

The Bandidos are also found in Australia; aside from the non-locale-specific Nomads chapter, the chapters are located in Adelaide, Ballarat, Brisbane (Bayside, Centro, City), Byron Bay, Cairns, Geelong, Gold Coast, Hunter Region, Port Stephens, Ipswich, Melbourne, Mid North Coast, Mid State, Mission Beach, Noosa, North Victoria, Northside, Sunshine Coast, Sydney, and Toowoomba, and were acquired with much bloodletting.

They have attempted to establish themselves in New Zealand starting in 2012. An attempt in South Auckland in 2012 was stymied when their main contact, a former member of the Highway 61 gang, was recalled to prison for meeting them. In 2013 it was reported that some former Highway 61 members in Christchurch had aligned with the Bandidos.

In Europe

The first European chapter opened in Marseilles in France in 1989, followed by chapters in Scandinavia, in Denmark in 1993 and Sweden in 1994. In recent years the club has also expanded heavily into Germany, Spain, Norway, Finland, Belgium, Italy, Netherlands, Luxembourg and the Channel Islands. As of March 15, 2014, the club has opened a new "Probationary Chapter" in Sittard, in the Netherlands. Additionally, it is looking into setting up shop in Russia and Eastern Europe and also in Singapore, Malaysia and Thailand. The Bandidos are organized by local chapters, with state and regional officers, as well as a national chapter made up of four regional vice presidents and a national president.

Support clubs

Like the Hells Angels, The Bandidos also have a number of "support" clubs, who are used as proxies for both legal and illegal activities.These groups usually wear reverse colors (gold border with red background rather than the Bandidos' red-border–and–gold background). They also commonly wear a unique patch (known as the "Heart Patch") consisting of a round patch in Bandidos colors on the front upper left of the colors (vest), as worn by the member. Most of these clubs are regional.

Criminal involvement

United States

In November 2006, Glenn Merritt of the Bellingham, Washington chapter was sentenced to four years in prison for drug possession and trafficking in stolen property. A total of 32 members were indicted in the associated investigation, on charges including conspiracy, witness tampering, and various drug and gun violations. Eighteen of those pled guilty. In October, 2006, George Wegers, then Bandidos' international president, pled guilty and received a two-year sentence for conspiracy to engage in racketeering.

On 16 August 2004, a passer-by on Interstate 10 flagged down a police car after finding Robert Quiroga, International Boxing Federation Super flyweight champion from 1990 to 1993, lying next to his car. Quiroga had been stabbed multiple times. Richard Merla, a member of the Bandidos, was arrested in 2006 for the killing and in 2007 pled no contest to murdering Quiroga; he was sentenced to 40 years in prison. "I don't regret it. I don't have no remorse. I don't feel sorry for him and his family. I don't and I mean that," Merla admits. In regards to the murder of Robert Quiroga, the Bandidos Motorcycle Club denounced any involvement in the crime, stating that Merla's actions were his own, and not those of the Club. Merla was expelled from the Bandidos due to his actions.

In March 2006 police in Austin, Texas announced that the Bandidos were the prime suspects in the March 18, 2006 slaying of a 44-year-old local motorcyclist named Anthony Benesh. Benesh, who had been trying to start an Austin chapter of the Hells Angels, was shot in the head by an unseen sniper, as he was leaving a North Austin restaurant with his girlfriend and two children. Police said that Benesh was flanked by other people and the shooter used only one bullet, fired at a distance from a high-powered rifle. The murder occurred on the same weekend as the annual Bandidos MC "Birthday Party" in Southeast Texas, marking the 40th anniversary of the club's 1966 founding. According to police, in the days before his murder, Benesh had been receiving telephone calls from Bandidos telling him to stop wearing a vest that displayed Hells Angels patches.

Scandinavia

A turf and drug war between the Hells Angels and the Bandidos, known as the "Great Nordic Biker War" raged from 1993 until 1997. It resulted in 11 murders, 74 attempted murders, and 96 wounded members of the involved biker clubs. In Denmark a law was passed in response to the biker war that banned biker clubs from owning or renting property for their club activities. The law was later repealed on constitutional grounds.

On 14 January 2009, the Bandidos Sweden President, Mehdi Seyyed, was sentenced to nine years in prison for two counts of attempted murder. He bombed two cars in Gothenburg, in September 2006, with hand grenades, in acts of revenge as the victims had previously testified against him. Four other Bandidos members received shorter sentences for their involvement in the attacks.

Australia

The Australian chapter was founded by Anthony Mark "Snodgrass" Spencer in 1983 following a split from the Comanchero Motorcycle Club. The Bandidos are known in Australia for their involvement in the Milperra Bikie Massacre, a shoot-out with the rival Comanchero Motorcycle Club that killed six gang members and a young bystander.

In 2002, a Bandidos Motorcycle Club member was shot and wounded by Sean Waygood and Michael Christiansen of the Anthony "Rooster" Perish criminal gang network in Haymarket, New South Wales

More recently, five Bandidos are accused of starting a blaze which destroyed the Rebels clubhouse at Albion, a suburb of Brisbane, Australia on 27 March 2007. All five faced Brisbane Magistrates Court again on 4 June 2007.

On 22 October 2008, Bandido member Ross Brand, 51 and an acquaintance were shot while walking outside the gang's Geelong clubhouse. Mr. Brand was struck in the head and died. Rival Rebels motorcycle gang affiliate John Russell Bedson was convicted for the shooting and sentenced to a maximum 23 years in jail, with an 18-year non-parole period

On 24 March 2009 the Sergeant at Arms of the Bandidos Parramatta chapter Mahmoud Dib was arrested and charged with firearms offences by police investigating a string of drive-by shootings in Sydney. Police found a .45 calibre semi-automatic pistol which was loaded with seven bullets. Days before Dib's arrest his family home was the scene of a wild shootout between members of the Bandidos and the Notorious gang in what is believed to be an ongoing feud with the latter Parramatta based bike group and the Bandidos.

On November 29, 2011 Toby Mitchell, 37, a Bandidos sergeant-at-arms and former champion heavyweight kickboxer, was fired on in Barkly Square shopping centre car park in Brunswick, Melbourne

On April 28, 2012, Jacques Teamo, a senior Bandidos member along with an innocent female by-stander received multiple gunshot wounds by a fellow gang member at the Robina Town Shopping Centre on the Gold Coast.

Bandidos clubhouse's and properties have been targeted by enemy gangs in the Brisbane Metropolitan Area, with the most recent incident being 2 drive-by shootings at the Bandidos Woolloongabba Clubhouse, and a Milton Tattoo Parlor in the early hours of June 4, 2012.

The club is also quite active on the Gold Coast.

Canada

Hells Angels Quebec president Maurice Boucher organized "puppet clubs" to persuade local Montreal, Quebec club Rock Machine-controlled bars, and their resident drug dealers, to surrender their illegal drug business. Rock Machine resistance led to bloodshed. On July 14, 1994, two members of the Hells Angels' top puppet club entered a downtown motorcycle shop and shot down a Rock Machine associate. That was the beginning of the Quebec Biker war.

That August, a Jeep wired with a remote-controlled bomb exploded killing a Rock Machine associate and an 11-year-old boy, Daniel Desrochers, who was playing in a nearby schoolyard. A month later, the first full Hells Angels member was shot to death entering his car at a shopping mall. Nine bombs went off around the province during his funeral.

The war eventually ended with mass killings by the Hells Angels, plus public outcry over the deaths of innocent bystanders resulted in police pressure including the incarceration of over 100 bikers.

It was this turf war that prompted the over-matched Rock Machine to align itself with the Bandidos patching over as Bandidos Quebec chapter. Not all members were happy about the patch-over. Some defected to other clubs while others remained with the club but hoped to restore their sovereignty.

Wayne Kellestine protests against
the London Ontario's gay pride parade
in 2005.

On April 8, 2006, four vehicles containing the bodies of
eight murdered men were discovered in a farmer's field
outside of the hamlet of Shedden, Ontario, Canada. Six of
the men killed in what became known as the Shedden
Massacre were full members of the Bandidos Toronto
branch, including the president of the organization in
Canada; they were Luis Manny Raposo, John Muscedere,
Jamie Flanz, George Jessome, George Kriarakis, Frank
Salerno, Paul Sinopoli and Michael Trotta. The suspects in
the case, Michael Sandham, Marcelo Aravena, Frank
Mather, Brett Gardiner, Dwight Mushey and Wayne
Kellestine, were also full members or probationary
members (also known as "prospects"), in what police
described as an internal cleansing of the Bandidos
organization NSCC (No Surrender Crew Canada). The
victims were brought to the farm of Kellestine, where they
were held captive before being systematically led out of his
barn and murdered "execution style."

On October 30, 2009 after eighteen hours of deliberation a jury in London, Ontario found the 6 suspects guilty on 44 counts of first degree murder and 4 counts of manslaughter.

These murders would finally close the chapter on the Bandidos Canada "No Surrender Crew" and end any hopes of Bandido dominance in the country. Many of the remaining Canadian Bandidos would later go on to re-form the Rock Machine Biker Gang in Canada early in 2008 which would spread outside their traditional home of Quebec and open up chapters in Australia and the United States.

Germany

Bandidos club house in Bochum, Germany

On June 11, 2008, two Bandidos members were convicted and sentenced to life imprisonment for the murder of a Hells Angels member in Ibbenbüren, Germany. Reports say they drove to his Harley-Davidson shop and shot him there on May 23, 2007. After the first day of a related lawsuit on

December 17, 2007, riots between the two gangs and the police had been reported. On October 8, 2009, a Bandidos member was shot to death by a Hells Angels prospect in Duisburg.

In February 2010, about 8 ethnic Turkish Bandido members and supporters in Berlin in an unprecedented move defected and joined the Hells Angels, forming a sub-chapter known as "Hells Angels Nomads Türkiye". This triggered a gang war in Berlin that lasted from February to April 2010.

On 26 April 2012 the authorities of North Rhine-Westphalia banned and disbanded the Aachen chapter of the Bandidos M.C., and three support clubs. In the following action carried out by the North Rhine-Westphalia Police 38 properties were searched, in which firearms and stabbing weapons were found. The display of Bandidos Symbols and the wearing of Bandidos Regalia was also forbidden in North Rhine-Westphalia. The Northrhine-Westphalia government found its actions necessary because the Bandidos wanted to build up their criminal supremacy through racketeering and violence.

Blue Angels Motorcycle Club

Motto: BAFFBA
Founded: 1963
Location: Glasgow, Scotland
Founder: Allan Morrison and Billy Gordon
Type: Outlaw motorcycle club
Region: UK, Belgium, Spain.
Activities: Oldest outlaw motorcycle club in Europe
Website: www.blueangelsscotland.com
Abbreviation: BAMC

The **Blue Angels Motorcycle Club** (**BAMC**) is a one-percenter motorcycle club that was formed by Allan Morrison and Billy Gordon in MARYHILL District of Glasgow Glasgow, Scotland in 1963. "Blue" stands for Bastards, Lunatics, Undesireables and Eccentrics but the name also came from other sources; blue is the main colour of the Scotland flag. The Blue Angels are one of the largest motorcycle clubs in the United Kingdom, only falling behind the Outlaws, Hells Angels and Satans Slaves

Clubhouse Blue Angels Belgium in Erpe

The Blue Angels have four chapters throughout Scotland and in Leeds The club's insignia consists of a skull wearing a German Army helmet (sometimes with a Swastika or a national flag on the side) and golden wings coming out from the side. John McDermot designed the patches and the name BLUE ANGELS came from a boat we saw in Loch Lomond in 1963.

The Breed Motorcycle Club

The Breed MC
Founded: 1960s
Founding location: Asbury Park, New Jersey, United States
Years active: 1960s-present
Territory: Chapters in New Jersey and Pennsylvania
Membership: 200
Criminal activities: Drug trafficking, extortion, robbery
Rivals: Hells Angels, Pagans and Warlocks

The Breed Motorcycle Club is a one-percenter
motorcycle gang that was formed 65 miles northeast of
Philadelphia in Asbury Park, New Jersey in 1965. It was at
one time one of the most powerful and feared biker gangs
in the Northeastern United States, with a number of
chapters in New Jersey and Pennsylvania. Although The
Breed were founded in the 1960s, the gang did not start to
expand rapidly until the early 1980s when members of the
Aces and Eights Motorcycle Club, based in Riverside, New
Jersey, patched over in 1983. In 1986, the Branded
Motorcycle Club was absorbed into The Breed. The Breed
headquarters was moved to Bristol Township,
Pennsylvania.

Criminal activities

In March 1971, The Breed were involved in a large-scale
brawl with the Hells Angels at a motorcycle show in
Cleveland, Ohio. Over a hundred bikers from both sides
were involved, and four members of The Breed and a Hells
Angel were stabbed to death. The fight had been planned
earlier. Dozens of vans and cars full of police officers were

called in to break up the fight. 57 bikers were arrested, but most fled.

Ten members of The Breed were arrested on the charges of extortion and rape on January 28, 2000. They had been running protection rackets on strip clubs, tattoo parlours and other businesses in Long Branch, New Jersey. The sexual assault charges were brought after four women, who danced at the clubs, complained to the Howell Township police. One woman said she had been chained to the floor for several days, forced to engage in oral sex with several men and beaten severely.

Three members of The Breed were arrested in July 2003 for beating up a former member of the club and various other charges. On October 5, 2002, Sanford Gorzelsky, Scott Lear and Frederick DeCapua allegedly attacked Arne "Ole" Olsen at the My Way Cafe in West Long Branch, New Jersey in retaliation for his testimony in a court case involving other Breed members. Scott Lear was acquitted of all charges except for conspiracy and Fredrick DeCapua was acquitted of all charges.

On July 21, 2006, fifteen members of The Breed were arrested for running a large scale crystal methamphetamine ring after a year-long investigation by the Attorney General's Bureau of Narcotics Investigation and the Philadelphia Police Department, known as "Operation Breed on a Wire". Among the indicted were Bristol PA chapter president John "Junior" Napoli, Jackson NJ "Mother" chapter president John "Shameless" Kovacs and 13 other club members. The Grand Jury found that Napoli was the ring leader of the drug organization operated in Pennsylvania and New Jersey, and distributed over 120 pounds of crystal methamphetamine from May 2005 through June 2006, which has an estimated street value of more than $11.25 million. Police also seized more than 22 pounds of crystal meth, nearly $500,000 in cash and bank deposits, 44 firearms (including one submachine gun), 10 improvised explosive devices, various vehicles and 24 motorcycles during a series of raids. Ultimately, John Kovacs and other club members were acquitted of all charges.

Brother Speed

Brother Speed MC

Founded: May 1969
Type: Outlaw motorcycle club
Region: Northwestern United States
Membership: 150
Website: brotherspeed.com

The **Brother Speed Motorcycle Club** is an outlaw motorcycle club that was formed in Boise, Idaho in 1969, but now has its mother chapter in Portland, Oregon. They are considered by Oregon's Department of Justice to be one of six "outlaw motorcycle gangs" in the state. Brother Speed is also listed as an "outlaw motorcycle club" by the Idaho Department of Corrections gang information web site.

Brother Speed was established by a group of high school friends who rode motorcycles together. The friends noticed an increase in motorcycles in the area and decided to run a newspaper ad looking for anyone interested in riding together and starting a motorcycle club. A meeting was organized with approximately 20 people attending the first meeting. A few weeks after the first meeting, the group came up with the name, "Brother Speed." The club's insignia is a winged skull with sunglasses and its "colors" are black and gold. There are around 150 Brother Speed members and there are eight chapters spread across Oregon, Idaho, Washington and Utah.

In 2006, a member was sentenced to 21 years for distributing methamphetamine and lying about it in court. In 2005, federal and local officers raided the then Brother Speed Clubhouse where it was believed many of the meth transactions had occurred. It was believed that the member was a major leader in a large meth trafficking ring.

On 19 September 2009, up to 26 motorcycles ridden by members of the Brother Speed motorcycle club were involved in a motorcycle crash on Interstate 5 near Wilsonville, Oregon. The crash inflicted serious injuries on two of the bikers, sending ten to the hospital, and closed off that portion of I-5 for four hours. One of the critically injured Brother Speed members improved and was released from the hospital; the other died as a result of injuries sustained in the crash.

The members of Brother Speed have a history of aggression and violence. In April 2012, 2 members of the BrotherSpeed Motorcycle Club were arrested on suspicion of harassment, menacing, reckless driving and recklessly endangering another person, among other charges. After chasing a car in Eugene, Or. They were reportedly hitting the car with their hands and a metal hook attached to a leather lash. In May 2012, 5 of the Idaho Falls members of Brothers Speed, attacked 2 members of Pocatello's Empties motorcycle club at a gathering put together for a small boy (Wesley Johnson) who was suffering from cancer, nearly 400 bikers gathered that Saturday to grant Wesley's wish to participate in a motorcycle rally.

Chosen Few MC

Chosen Few MC

Motto: Give none, take none
Founded: 1959
Location: South Central, Los Angeles
Founder: Lionel, Lil Frank, Roger, Hawk, Slim, Shirly Bates, and Champ
Leader: Fontayne
Type: Outlaw motorcycle club
Region: USA and Philippines
Membership: 2,000 members, 15 Chapters
Website: www.chosenfewmc.org
Abbreviation: CF, 36, CFMC

The **Chosen Few MC** were the first racially integrated outlaw motorcycle club established by Lionel Ricks in Los Angeles, California in 1959. Originally an African-American motorcycle club, its first white member joined in 1960.

Other clubs

The same name is used by other unrelated motorcycle clubs in Iowa, New York, Belgium, Ireland, and Canada.

Comanchero Motorcycle Club

Comanchero MC

Founded: 1965 or 1973
Location: Sydney, Australia
Founder: William George "Jock" Ross
Type: Outlaw motorcycle club
Region: New South Wales coast
Membership: 100

The **Comanchero Motorcycle Club** is an outlaw motorcycle gang in Australia, with chapters in Strathfield. The word *outlaw* itself carries a specific meaning which does not imply immediate criminal intent; rather it means the club is not sanctioned by the American Motorcyclist Association (AMA) and does not adhere to the AMA's rules. The Comancheros are participants in the United

Motorcycle Council of NSW, which has recently convened a conference aimed at addressing legislation aimed against the "bikie" clubs, their poor public image in the wake of several violent clashes and ongoing biker wars, and defusing deadly feuds such as the Comancheros' battles with the Hells Angels. The sincerity of these efforts to defend the battered image of the clubs has met with skepticism.

History

The original club was formed by William George "Jock" Ross, a Scottish immigrant, in Sydney, New South Wales in 1968. He chose the name after seeing the John Wayne film *The Comancheros*. In late 1982, a second Comanchero chapter was formed by Anthony Mark "Snoddy" Spencer, who had broken away from the first chapter after challenging Ross' authority. When visiting the United States with Charles Paul "Charlie" Scibberas, another member of the second chapter, Spencer met with members of the Texan motorcycle club, the Bandidos and the two gangs became allies. The Bandidos eventually patched-over the second Comanchero chapter to become the Bandidos' first Australian chapter.

The Comanchero and Bandidos were now rivals and in 1984, the two clubs were involved in the Milperra massacre, a shoot-out which left seven people dead, including four Comanchero, two Bandidos, and a 14-year-old bystander. Jock Ross received a lifetime jail sentence for his involvement in the Milperra massacre but only served five years and three months before he was released.

The Comanchero and Hells Angels were also believed to be involved in a clash at Sydney Airport on Sunday, 22 March

2009. The clash resulted in one man being beaten to death and police estimated as many as 15 men were involved in the violence. Police documents detail the brawl as a result of a Comanchero Club member and a Hells Angels Member being on the same flight from Melbourne. Six Comancheros were arrested as a result of the altercation and have been convicted of "riot and affray", while Comanchero president Mick Hawi was also found guilty of murder on 2 November 2011. As a result of heightening violence, New South Wales Premier Nathan Rees announced the state police anti-gang squad would be boosted to 125 members from 50.

It was announced in late 2009 that a new national president was elected named Duax Ngakuru.

Perth chapter

The Comanchero established a single Western Australian chapter in 2010 which is presently located on Wellman Street, Northbridge at the Fitness and Fight Centre.

The Comanchero expansion into Western Australia was delayed by the 2010 arrest of Steve Milenkovski who was about to be patched as the Perth's Chapter president when he was arrested in the culmination of Operation Baystone. Operation Baystone resulted in Milenkovski, Yavuz Ozan, Hao Bi, and Mark Vick Kitos being charged with various drug offences. The operation seized 7.5 kilograms of methylamphetamine imported into Western Australia from New South Wales.

In August 2012 Milenkovski was found guilty of two counts of Possess a Prohibited Drug with Intent to Sell or Supply after a 9 week Perth District Court trial and faces a long term of imprisonment when sentenced. Two of his co-accused, were convicted of one charge each of attempted possession. Hao Bi, who was alleged to have been the courier was acquitted.

In September 2012 Milenkovski was sentenced to 17 years jail as the "king pin" behind the scheme. David Tanevski was sentenced to eight years' jail, in the District Court of WA.

Infighting

On 5 September 2012, Comanchero member Faalau Pisu was murdered, being shot in the head outside the Serbian National Defence Council at Canley Vale whilst attending a wedding. A 25-year-old gang member and a 27-year-old associate of the club were also shot and injured. NSW Police allege that an internal rift within the Comanchero was behind recent shootings involving Comanchero members.

Devils Diciples

Devils Diciples MC

Founded: 1967
Location: Fontana, California, United States
Type: Outlaw motorcycle club
Region: USA
Membership:150
Website: www.devilsdiciples.org
Abbreviation: DDMC

The **Devils Diciples Motorcycle Club (DDMC)** is an outlaw motorcycle club that was founded in Fontana, California in 1967. The word *outlaw* carries a specific meaning which does not imply criminal intent, but rather means the club is not sanctioned by the American

Motorcyclist Association (AMA) and does not adhere to the AMA's rules. The club originally had twelve members, and the word "disciples" was intentionally misspelled. Their insignia is a motorcycle wheel with two tridents crossing over it. In the United States, the club has chapters in Alabama, Arizona, California, Illinois, Indiana, Michigan, Mississippi and Ohio. The headquarters of the club are in Clinton Charter Township, Michigan, Port Huron, Michigan, and Detroit and there are around 150 full-patched members in the club.

Controversies

Since 1995, a number of members of the club have been accused or convicted of selling or manufacturing illegal substances. Hells Angels member John R. Bartolomeo is serving 35 years in prison for the June 29, 1995 murder of Devils Diciples member William "Cats" Michaels. US Drug Enforcement Administration (DEA) agent Phil Muollo, who infiltrated the Hells Angels, said that Bartolomeo was a "prospect" (prospective member) of the Hells Angels, and that he killed the rival gang member to prove that he was worthy to be a full member of the Hells Angels.

In November 2006, the U.S. District Court in Detroit closed its first major meth case with the sentencing of two Devils Diciples members and five associates in connection to manufacturing methamphetamine.

In an investigation into the club begun in 2002, prosecutors have recently requested dropping the last remaining charges against the club's national president, Jeff "Fat Dog" Garvin Smith, "to avoid compromising an ongoing investigation and because the interests of justice require it."

Charges against 17 other club members or associates had been dropped in April. These charges included drug trafficking and other offenses, brought when 18 alleged members of the Devils Diciples were arrested on April 2, 2009 by the Federal Bureau of Investigation. During the raid, 42 firearms, 3,000 rounds of ammunition, three bullet-proof vests, $12,000, 15 casino-style slot machines, 1,000 Vicodin and OxyContin pills, 1½ pounds of methamphetamine and 55 pounds of marijuana were seized. The remaining charges Smith was to be tried for were being "a violent felon in possession of body armor" as well as "using a communications facility (a telephone) in furtherance of drug trafficking".

New Baltimore, Michigan District Court Judge Paul Cassidy was investigated in April 2009 for allegedly giving Devils Diciples members preferential treatment. He is a boyhood friend of their National President Jeff Garvin Smith. Cassidy announced his retirement after his home and office were searched as part of the investigation of the Devils Diciples. In 2011, Stephen J. Kinzey, a kinesiology professor at California State University, San Bernardino, was accused of smuggling methamphetamine while part of the gang.

Duane "Dog" Chapman, now an anti-crime celebrity bounty hunter, was associated with the club during his adolescence.

July 2012, 31 Devils Diciples members in Michigan and Alabama were arrested by the FBI. More than 60 firearms and more than 6,000 rounds of ammunition were seized during this investigation. In addition, eight methamphetamine manufacturing laboratories were dismantled.

Diablos Motorcycle Club

Diablos Motorcycle club

Founded: 1961
Location: San Bernardino, California
Founder: John J. "Jack" Baltas, Snr.
Type: Outlaw motorcycle club
Region: USA

The **Diablos Motorcycle Club** is a "one-percenter" outlaw motorcycle club that has chapters in cities across the United States.

On September 24, 1998, Diablo club member Raymond "Stoney" Stone and seven other members were charged with various crimes (including Stone's confession in his involvement in the 1992 murder of rival gang member Mike D'Amato of Wallingford, Connecticut's James Gang MC for which he would be sentenced to 20 years imprisonment).

Keith Gallagher, the vice president of the Diablos' national chapter, was indicted on charges of cocaine trafficking on January 24, 2006.

Diablos member Jerry Louis Fantauzzi was arrested on December 7, 2005, following a long-term investigation into the Diablos in Waterbury and Meriden, Connecticut. On November 20, 2006, he was sentenced to ten years imprisonment on charges of drug dealing.

On April 22, 2012, the national leader and founder of the Diablos, Jack Baltas, died at the age of 70, two days after being released from prison. Although incarcerated for trafficking drugs, Baltas was known for his good work and kind deeds in his home town of Meriden, Connecticut, buying lunch for the needy and helping neighbors with chores.

El Forastero Motorcycle Club

El Forastero MC

Founded1962

Location: Sioux City, Iowa
Founder: Tom Fugle and Harlan "Tiny" Brower
Key people: David Mann
Type: Outlaw motorcycle club
Region: Midwestern USA
Membership:100
Website: www.elforasteromc.net

El Forastero Motorcycle Club (EFMC) is a one-percenter motorcycle club which was established after being turned down for a chapter by the Satan Slaves MC. The El Forasteros are well known for their criminal activities, and are considered by law enforcement to be among the many second-tier, after the "Big Four" gangs, outlaw motorcycle gangs operated as organized crime enterprises.

Its early members included the renowned biker artist Dave Mann. The name of the club means "the outsider" in Spanish.

The club was founded in 1962 by Tom Fugle and Harlan "Tiny" Brower has chapters in Iowa, Minnesota, Kansas, and Missouri and close links to the Galloping Goose MC.

Some of the club members have been found guilty for the crimes motorcycle theft and for transporting and distributing methamphetamine after members testified the club members pooled money to buy narcotics for consumption at their organized events.

El Forastero member William Eneff received a sentence of seven years in federal prison without parole after pleading guilty conspiracy to distribute methamphetamine. According to the US Department of Justice, Eneff, "admitted that members of El Forastero and the affiliated Galloping Goose Motorcycle Club were required to annually pay dues and attend a certain number of motorcycle trips, known as runs, each year. On each run, the members were required to pay money that was pooled, or collected by each club charter, then forwarded to the specific Galloping Goose or El Forastero charter that hosted the particular motorcycle run in order to purchase methamphetamine, cocaine and marijuana. Those drugs were maintained in run bags, which were distributed to all club members who attended the run."

An editorial by Mark Sheehan in the St. Joseph News-Press expressed wonderment at the advanced age of the "dangerous motorcycle gang", the El Forasteros, noting that among one group indicted on methamphetamine charges in 2006, "the ages of these rebels on wheels range from 51 to 60". Indicted El Forastero Larry D. "Eight Ball" Williams was at age 60 a "card-carrying member of AARP." Sheehan said, "My deepest concern is that we are stuck in a psychological rut. We are determined to live in the 1960s when motorcycle gangs were cool."

Finks motorcycle club

Finks Motorcycle Club

Motto: Attitude Violence
Founded: 1969
Location: Sydney
Type: Outlaw motorcycle club
Region: Australia

The **Finks** is an Australian outlaw motorcycle club that was formed in Sydney Australia, in 1969 and now also has chapters in other states. The name comes from The Wizard of Id cartoon where the peasants, to his dismay, often proclaim, "The King is a fink!". The logo used by the Finks is of Bung, the king's jester. The pants worn by the jester differ in colour depending on the state the chapter resides in. The Macquarie dictionary defines a Fink as "someone who betrays his or her associates, as an informer".

The club was restricted by government actions in South Australia. Despite rivalries, various other groups joined together to protest the South Australian government's proposed restrictions.

It was reported in October 2013 that most members were to switch to the United States based Mongols Motorcycle Club.

Perth chapter

The Perth chapter of the Finks were formed after Troy Mercanti was expelled from the Coffin Cheaters and joined his friend and South Australian Fink member Frank Condo in forming the Perth chapter in 2008. Other eastern states members came to Perth to start the chapter, but over time all, including Condo, either left the club or returned to their original states. The commencement of the Perth chapter caused friction between the Finks and the Coffin Cheaters Perth, culminating in a violent brawl at the Perth Motorplex in October 2010.

The Perth Finks clubhouse has been frozen under the proceeds of crime after Mercanti's then partner Tammy Kingdon was convicted by a District Court jury in November 2010 of four counts of stealing and one count of property laundering. Kingdon funnelled money from a Coffin Cheaters trust fund set up for the daughters of Marc Chabriere, who was a Coffin Cheaters member murdered during the 1998 bikie war between the Coffin Cheaters and the Club Deroes. The stolen money from the fund was used to purchase the Finks clubhouse.

During the Motorplex brawl Fink member Stephen Wallace had three fingers severed by a knife, and Fink member David Marrapodi suffered a gunshot wound to the leg.Following the Motorplex incident an Australian Crime Commission hearing was held calling both members of the Finks and the Coffin Cheaters. As a result of the hearings convictions for contempt were recorded in late 2010 against Finks members Clovis Chikonga, Troy Smith, Stephen Laurence Silvestro, Tristan Roger Allbeury, and Stephen Wallace. All were imprisoned for two years despite pleas from their lawyer who claimed the likes of Allbeury were bipolar, had ADHD and suffered post-traumatic stress.

Wallace is the long term boyfriend of fellow convicted heroin trafficker Holly Deane-Johns, who served time in WA before arrest in Thailand in 2000 for trying to mail 10.4 grams of heroin to Perth. She was jailed in 2003 for 31 years before her prisoner transfer deal in 2007.

Allbeury is currently held on remand after being charged by Gang Crime Squad Detectives with Attempting to Pervert the Course of Justice. Allbeury is also charged with Grievous Bodily Harm over a prison assault that broke a fellow inmates jaw. In September 2012, whilst in prison, Allbeury was found with a smart phone and cannabis in his cell.

Mercanti was arrested in January 2012 by the Gang Crime Squad and jailed in March 2013 for 6 years and 10 months after pleading guilty late in his trial to domestic violence charges against his former partner Tammy Kingdon. Increasing drug and alcohol use were blamed for the 15 years of abuse. During the trial Kingdon was examined about drug use and about sex between her, Mercanti and fellow Fink member Josh Luke Rider and his partner Justine Rider. Josh Rider is currently held on remand after being charged by the Gang Crime Squad, in early 2013, with drunk driving, minor drug offences and having a loaded handgun concealed inside his motor bike.

In October 2013 the Perth Finks were patched over to the Mongols MC.

Eastern states chapters

In 2012, Finks member Mark James Graham was charged with the attempted murder of Bandidos member Jacques Teamo in a shooting at the Robina Town Centre shopping centre

In 2012, Patrick Mcmillan was arrested and charged with firing a pistol at a man, and intentionally and recklessly causing serious injury to him at his Ferntree Gully home he shared with his girlfriend Rachel Osborn, theft, trespass, drug and weapon possession, dealing with proceeds of crime and traffic offences.

Free Souls Motorcycle Club

Free Souls MC

Founded: 1968
Type: Outlaw motorcycle club
Region: Oregon and Washington states
Website: www.free-souls-motorcycle-club.com

The **Free Souls Motorcycle Club** is a one-percenter motorcycle club that was formed in Eugene, Oregon in 1968. The club has over 100 members and there are a number of club chapters throughout the U.S. state of

Oregon and a single chapter in Vancouver, Washington, Australia, and Germany. The club's insignia is an ankh, the ancient Egyptian symbol of eternal life, and their "colors" are blue and white.

Criminal activities

Three Free Souls members were arrested on a number of charges on May 2, 2007, after the Bureau of Alcohol, Tobacco, Firearms and Explosives and local police raided six homes in Eugene. Ten stolen motorcycles, guns, methamphetamine, marijuana and hashish oil were seized.

Galloping Goose Motorcycle Club

Galloping Goose MC

Motto: "Often Tested, Always Faithful"
Founded: 1942
Location: Los Angeles, California
Founder: Dick Hershberg
Type: Outlaw motorcycle club
Region: Midwestern USA
Website: www.galloping-goosemc.com
Abbreviation: GG Bunch

Galloping Goose Motorcycle Club (**GGMC**) is a one-percenter motorcycle club that began around a motorcycle racing team and friends based out of Los Angeles, California in the United States in 1942. The group was informal and not chartered until 1946. Soon after, the organization spread out from southern California, establishing chapters in Illinois, Missouri, Montana, Indiana, Wyoming, Kansas, Mississippi, and Louisiana.

Members of the Galloping Goose MC were at the 1947 Hollister Rally which was the basis for the 1954 film *The Wild One*. This led to the beginning of the highly visible and structured 1% or outlaw motorcycle clubs, along with the Boozefighters MC when the AMA forbade club members to participate in AMA events unless they took off their patches.

The club has a close relationship with El Forastero Motorcycle Club.

An expert on outlaw motorcycle gangs from Missouri State Highway Patrol said the Galloping Goose were expanding into territory formerly controlled by the Pharaohs motorcycle club during the 1980s and 1990s. He described them as a "one percenter club", which took over another club, the Midwest Drifters, and uses them to run errands and provide cash. He said Galloping Goose's rules of behavior sometimes include violent crimes.

Gremium Motorcycle Club

Gremium Motorcycle Club

Founded: 1972
Location: Mannheim, Germany
Type: Outlaw motorcycle club
Region: Europe
Website: www.gremium.de

A European rider with a Gremium patch

Gremium Motorcycle Club is a German outlaw motorcycle club. Gremium claims to be the largest German motorcycle club with 73 full chapters in Germany, 71 chapters in other European countries, several associate chapters (Bad 7 MC support club) in Germany, and a prospect chapter opened by German expatriates in Pattaya, Thailand in 2007. The club was established in 1972 in Mannheim.

The club colors are black and white, on the back patch appears the word "GREMIUM" and the name of the country with a fist rising through clouds. Often, the terms "Black Seven" and the number 7 are used: the word "Gremium" consists of seven letters, and "G" is the seventh letter in the alphabet.

Criminal investigations and sanctions

The society as a whole was prohibited on 10 November 1988 by the Ministry of the Interior of Baden-Württemberg as a criminal organization.

At the time of confrontation with the Mannheim judiciary, the bylaws were closely based on the Mannheim *Studentenverbindung* (student society or fraternity) "Hermunduria" in which the then President Michael "Mike" Heyer had been a member as a law student. Unaware of its origins, the prosecutor accused of forming a criminal association among other things. In subsequent criminal proceedings ordered by the District Court of Mannheim, the prosecution accused certain members of the club of crimes. The prosecutor, whose club informant turned out to be unreliable in court, had the charge of forming a criminal organization then fail.

On 16 January 1992, the club ban was lifted by the Administrative Court of Baden-Württemberg. Despite appropriate investigative efforts of the authorities,[6] since it came only to convictions of individual members only and not as a renewed accusation against such a club.

Gremium is regularly listed among other large motorcycle clubs, for example in the Annual Report on the Protection of the Constitution on Bavaria. In these reports, the body, with other mentioned motorcycle clubs associated with it, is associated with human trafficking, illegal prostitution, drug and/or weapons trafficking and organized crime. According to the German Federal Criminal Police Office in 2010, there were five organized crime investigation with respect to Gremium.

According to German Criminal Police, the group was involved in battles with the rival Bandidos Motorcycle Club in Scandinavia during the 1990s, which escalated to the use of bombs and grenade launchers.

Racing sponsorship

Gremium is a sponsor of the Black 7 Racing Team top fuel dragbike, along with more traditional corporate sponsors such as DeWalt Tools.

Grim Reapers Motorcycle Club (Canada)

Grim Reapers MC

Grim Reapers Motorcycle Club, Alberta colours

Founding location: Alberta, Canada
Years active: 1967-1997
Territory: Western Canada
Criminal activities: Drug trafficking, murder, assault, extortion
Allies: Hells Angels, Rebels
Rivals: Kings Crew, Rebels, Outcasts, Warlords, RCMP

The **Grim Reapers Motorcycle Club** was an outlaw motorcycle club, founded in 1967 in Calgary, Alberta, that was active during the sixties and seventies, and grew to become a dominant club in the region during the eighties and nineties.

They were apparently independent of a US-based motorcycle club of the same name that was founded in 1965 in Louisville, Kentucky. Along with the *Rebels*, the *Warlords*, and *King's Crew*, they were one of the four dominant outlaw motorcycle clubs operating in Alberta prior to 1997. In 1997, the club became part of the Hells Angels in a patch-over ceremony held in Red Deer, Alberta.

In 1970, 11 members and 2 associates were sentenced to life in prison for the murder of Ronald Hartley, president of the Outcasts Motorcycle Club. After an appeal several members were released and others had their sentences reduced. Two members were eventually convicted and sentenced to life in prison for the murder.

The Grim Reapers were listed as an "Outlaw Motorcycle Gang" by Criminal Intelligence Service Canada.In 1997, primarily because of public outcry due to escalating violence in eastern Canada between the Rock Machine and the Hells Angels' Quebec chapters, the Canadian government passed Bill C-95 which amended the Criminal Code of Canada (and other legislation) to give Canadian law enforcement organizations powers similar to those provided to their American counterparts via RICO.

Several former members of the Reapers, later to become members of the Hells Angels' Western Canadian chapters, were eventually successful in their challenge of charges brought against them under the new legislation as a result of events that occurred in relation to their patch-over gathering in Red Deer. In 2005, the bikers in Alberta won a major court victory when a judge ruled that police violated their constitutional rights during a roadside check in 1997.

Gypsy Joker Motorcycle Club

Gypsy Joker MC

Gypsy Joker colors (left) with members of other outlaw clubs at the Gypsy Jokers Protest Run, 14 March 2009

Founded: April 1, 1956
Founding location: San Francisco, California
Years active: 1956-present
Territory: Australia, Germany, South Africa, Norway and the United States
Criminal activities: Armed robbery, arson, assault, counterfeiting, drug trafficking, fraud, gun trafficking, homicide, identity theft, motorcycle theft, prostitution
Rivals: Mongols

The **Gypsy Joker Motorcycle Club (GJMC)**, or the **Gypsy Jokers** as they are called in Australia, are a "one-percenter" motorcycle gang and organized crime syndicate that was originally formed in San Francisco, California on April Fool's Day, 1956. They are one of the most notorious and violent motorcycle gangs in both the US and in Australia.

Prominently featured in Hunter Thompson's book *Hell's Angels: The Strange and Terrible Saga of the Outlaw Motorcycle Gangs*, they were the second most powerful outlaw motorcycle club in California until they were forced out of the San Francisco Bay Area by the Hells Angels. They relocated to Oregon and Washington in 1967, taking up temporary residence in Lincoln City, Oregon. The club has since spread to Australia, Germany, Norway and South Africa. There are approximately 35 chapters worldwide. In response to proposed anti-"bikie" laws in Australia, a protest rally was held in 2009, including a show of support by many other outlaw bikers, even among rival gangs.

Australia

The group has a high profile in Australia, especially in the southern and western regions. They are well known in Australia for the 2001 car bomb murder of Western Australia's former chief detective Don Hancock. The gang had an altercation with Hancock at the hotel he owned in Kalgoorlie. After setting up a campsite Gypsy Joker Billy Grierson
was shot dead by a sniper and it was alleged that Hancock was the shooter.

Gypsy Joker club members claimed that on January 12, 2001, a member was severely beaten by police in Adelaide, South Australia for refusing to remove his motorcycle helmet and sunglasses.

In February 2008, police forced the Gypsy Jokers to dismantle its clubhouse fortifications, which include a concrete front wall, surveillance cameras and modified doors, in Perth, Western Australia. The club said the security was needed in the area where the burglary rate is high.

Two Gypsy Joker members were jailed on March 5, 2009 on charges of assault. On May 12, 2007, Dean Alan Adams and Peter Floyd Robinson attacked Petera Heta Haimona outside the Cactus Club in Gosnells, Western Australia and beat him with metal pipes.

A Gypsy Joker was charged with unlawful possession a large sum of cash, weapons and ammunition on August 17, 2007. Police pulled his car over and discovered a gun, an expandable baton, capsicum spray and ammunition when they searched his vehicle.

A Gypsy Joker member was charged with attempted murder on March 17, 2009. He shot and wounded a member of the Newboys gang and former Hells Angel outside their clubhouse in Adelaide, South Australia.

On May 19, 2009, five Gypsy Jokers were involved in a drug-related shoot-out with another gang in Perth, Western Australia. Two were wounded and taken to hospital, one of which was Club President Leonard Mark Kirby.

On April 14, 2012, Gypsy Joker Anthony "Rooster" Perish, his brother Andrew (a Rebels Motorcycle Club gang member) and Matthew Lawton were sentenced to eighteen, nine and fifteen years respectively for the murder of convicted drug trafficker Terry Falconer, conspiracy to commit murder and firearms and drug offences

United States

In 2004, the police raided the Gypsy Joker clubhouse in Portland, Oregon looking for two men wanted for armed robbery. The men were not there, however, and the club sued the Portland Police Bureau for $50,000 because of the damage caused in the raid.[17]

On April 10, 2008, police raided the Gypsy Joker clubhouse in Kennewick, Washington and arrested four men for possession of methamphetamine. Stolen property and weapons were also seized from the premises.

On August 13, 2009, police in Nampa, Idaho, with assistance of the FBI, pulled over and detained approximately 60 to 70 members of the Gypsy Joker MC just off exit 38 on interstate 84. They were searched, interrogated, and photographed for future reference by law enforcement concerning gang affiliated activity.

On October 12, 2013 Joshua Cavett a member of the Gypsy Jokers allegedly murdered his estranged wife in front of her two daughters and kidnapped the youngest daughter. He has been arraigned and is currently set for trial for charges of aggravated murder, burglary and felon in possession of a firearm. Cavvett is likely to face the death penalty for these charges.

Hangmen Motorcycle Club

Hangmen Motorcycle Club

Founded: 1960s
Location: Richmond, California
Founder: Ray Aho
Type: Outlaw motorcycle club
Region: USA, Germany
Website: www.hangmenmc.org

The **Hangmen Motorcycle Club** is an outlaw motorcycle club founded in Richmond, California in 1960. The word *outlaw* carries a specific meaning which does not necessarily imply criminal intent, but rather means the club is not sanctioned by the American Motorcyclist Association (AMA) and does not adhere to the AMA's rules, but instead, generally, the club enforces a set of bylaws on its members that derive from the values of the outlaw biker culture The colors are black and gold, and the logo is a noose, they have Chapters all over the Western US and one in Germany.

Hangmen MC is a registered trademark with the United States Patent and Trademark Office.

Hangmen MC was established by a group of friends who rode motorcycles together. With the increase of outlaw motorcycle clubs in the State of California, they decided to establish their own motorcycle club and make their mark in history. Founder Ray Aho named the club Hangmen MC. There were 12 charter members when the club was formed.

Biker artist David Mann, an illustrator renown for his work for a motorcycle magazine called Easyriders created three paintings about the Hangmen Motorcycle Club: "Untitled" "Tijuana Jail Break", and "El Forastero New Year's Party".

Head Hunters MC

Head Hunters Motorcycle Club

Founded: 1967
Years active: 1967-present
Territory: West Auckland, Wellsford, Northland
Criminal activities: Drug Dealing, rape, theft, murder
Allies: Hells Angels, Black Power

The **Head Hunters Motorcycle Club** is an outlaw motorcycle club in New Zealand. It was formed in around 1967. The club has been tied to West Auckland throughout its existence. It is one of the fastest growing clubs, and second most dangerous after the Mongrel Mob.

Head Hunters members have been charged with various crimes including rape, theft, drug dealing, and murder.

The Head Hunters have chapters in Auckland, Wellsford, Northland, and Wellington.

Fight Club

The Head Hunters have a fight club which has been visited by famous people like Mark Hunt and Ali Cambell.

Hells Angels

Hells Angels MC

Motto: "When we do right, nobody remembers. When we do wrong, nobody forgets"
Founded: March 17, 1948
Key people: Sonny Barger
Type: Outlaw motorcycle club
Region: Worldwide (230 chapters in 27 countries)
Website: www.hells-angels.com
Abbreviation: HA, 81, HAMC

The **Hells Angels Motorcycle Club (HAMC)** is a worldwide one-percenter motorcycle club whose members typically ride Harley-Davidson motorcycles and is considered an organized crime syndicate by the U.S. Department of Justice. In the United States and Canada, the Hells Angels are incorporated as the **Hells Angels Motorcycle Corporation**. Common nicknames for the club are the "H.A.", "Red & White", and "81" (H and A being the eighth and first letters of the alphabet).

History

The Hells Angels were originally started by American war immigrants, the Bishop family in Fontana, California followed by an amalgamation of former members from different motorcycle clubs, such as the Pissed Off Bastards of Bloomington. The Hells Angels' website denies the suggestion that any misfit or malcontent troops are connected with the motorcycle club. The website also notes that the name was suggested by Arvid Olsen, an associate of the founders, who had served in the Flying Tigers' "Hells Angels" squadron in China during World War II. The name "Hells Angels" was inspired by the typical naming of American squadrons, or other fighting groups, with a fierce, death-defying title in both World War I and World War II, e.g., the Flying Tigers (American Volunteer Group) in Burma and China fielded three squadrons of P-40s and the third Squadron was called "Hell's Angels". In 1930, the Howard Hughes film *Hell's Angels* displayed extraordinary and dangerous feats of aviation, and it is believed that the World War II groups who used that name based it on the film.

Some of the early history of the HAMC is not clear, and accounts differ. According to Ralph 'Sonny' Barger, founder of the Oakland chapter, early chapters of the club were founded in San Francisco, Gardena, Fontana, as well as his chapter in Oakland, and other places independently of one another, with the members usually being unaware that there were other Hells Angels clubs. One of lesser known clubs existed in North Chino/South Pomona, CA Late 1960s-as late as1970.

Other sources claim that the Hells Angels in San Francisco were originally organized in 1953 by Rocky Graves, a Hells Angel member from San Bernardino ("Berdoo") implying that the "Frisco" Hells Angels were very much aware of their forebears. The "Frisco" Hells Angels were reorganized in 1955 with thirteen charter members, Frank Sadilek serving as President, and using the smaller, original logo. The Oakland chapter, at the time headed by Barger used a larger version of the "Death's Head" patch nicknamed the "Barger Larger" which was first used in 1959. It later became the club standard.

The Hells Angels are often depicted in a similarly mythical fashion as other modern-day legends like the James-Younger Gang; free-spirited, iconic, bound by brotherhood and loyalty. At other times, such as in the 1966 Roger Corman film *The Wild Angels* where they are depicted as violent and nihilistic, they are portrayed as a violent criminal gang and a scourge on society.

The club became prominent within, and established its initial notoriety as part of, the 1960s counterculture movement in San Francisco's Haight-Ashbury scene, London, in England, and elsewhere where it played a part at many of the movement's seminal events. Original members were directly connected to many of the counterculture's primary leaders, such as Ken Kesey and the Merry Pranksters, Allen Ginsberg, Jerry Garcia and The Grateful Dead, Timothy Leary, The Beatles, The Rolling Stones, Mick Farren and Tom Wolfe. The club launched the career of "Gonzo" journalist Hunter S. Thompson.

Criminologist Karen Katz said in 2011 that the Hells Angels were the center of a moral panic in Canada involving the media, politicians, law enforcement and the public that sensationalized the importance of isolated criminal acts.

Criminal activities and incidents

Main article: Hells Angels MC criminal allegations and incidents

Numerous police and intelligence agencies internationally classify the Hells Angels as one of the "big four" motorcycle gangs, along with the Pagans, Outlaws, and Bandidos, and contend that members carry out widespread violent crimes, drug dealing, trafficking in stolen goods and extortion and are involved in the prostitution industry. Members of the organization have continuously asserted that they are only a group of motorcycle enthusiasts who have joined to ride motorcycles together, to organize social events such as group road trips, fundraisers, parties, and motorcycle rallies and that those crimes are the responsibility of the individuals who carried them out and not the club as a whole. Members of the club have been accused of crimes and convicted in many host nations.

Insignia

Insignia of the Hells Angels from Karlsruhe chapter, with the '1%' patch

The Hells Angels' official website attributes the official "death's head" insignia design to Frank Sadilek, past president of the San Francisco Chapter. The colors and shape of the early-style jacket emblem (prior to 1953) were copied from the insignias of the 85th Fighter Squadron and the 552nd Medium Bomber Squadron.

The Hells Angels utilize a system of patches, similar to military medals. Although the specific meaning of each patch is not publicly known, the patches identify specific or significant actions or beliefs of each biker. The official colors of the Hells Angels are red lettering displayed on a white background—hence the club's nickname "The Red and White". These patches are worn on leather or denim jackets and vests.

Red and white are also used to display the number 81 on many patches, as in "Support 81, Route 81". The 8 and 1 stand for the respective positions in the alphabet of *H* and *A*. These are used by friends and supporters of the club, in deference to club rules which purport to restrict the wearing of Hells Angels imagery to club members.

The diamond-shaped one-percenter patch is also used, displaying '1%', in red on a white background with a red merrowed border. The term one-percenter is said to be a response to the American Motorcyclist Association (AMA) comment on the Hollister incident, to the effect that 99% of motorcyclists were law-abiding citizens and the last 1% were outlaws. The AMA has no record of such a statement to the press, and calls this story apocryphal.

New York Hells Angels patch.

Most members wear a rectangular patch (again, white background with red letters and a red merrowed border) identifying their respective chapter locations. Another similarly designed patch reads "Hells Angels". When applicable, members of the club wear a patch denoting their position or rank within the organization. The patch is rectangular, and, similarly to the patches described above, displays a white background with red letters and a red merrowed border. Some examples of the titles used are President, Vice President, Secretary, Treasurer, and Sergeant at Arms. This patch is usually worn above the 'club location' patch. Some members also wear a patch with the initials "AFFA", which stands for "Angels Forever;

Forever Angels", referring to their lifelong membership in the biker club (i.e., "once a member, always a member").

The book *Gangs*, written by Tony Thompson (a crime correspondent for *The Observer*), states that Stephen Cunningham, a member of the Angels, sported a new patch after he recovered from attempting to set a bomb: two Nazi-style SS lightning bolts below the words 'Filthy Few'. Some law enforcement officials claim that the patch is only awarded to those who have committed, or are prepared to commit, murder on behalf of the club. According to a report from the *R. v. Bonner and Lindsay* case in 2005 *(see related section below)*, another patch, similar to the 'Filthy Few' patch, is the 'Dequiallo' patch. This patch "signifies that the wearer has fought law enforcement on arrest". There is no common convention as to where the patches are located on the members' jacket/vest.

Intellectual property rights

In March 2007, the Hells Angels filed suit against the Walt Disney Motion Pictures Group alleging that the film entitled *Wild Hogs* used both the name and distinctive logo of the Hells Angels Motorcycle Corporation without permission. The suit was eventually voluntarily dismissed, after it received assurances from Disney that its references would not appear in the film.

In October 2010, the Hells Angels filed a lawsuit against Alexander McQueen for "misusing its trademark winged death heads symbol" in several items from its Autumn/Winter 2010 collection. The lawsuit is also aimed at Saks Fifth Avenue and Zappos.com, which stock the jacquard box dress and knuckle duster ring which bear the symbol which has been used since at least 1948 and is protected by the U.S. Patent and Trademark Office. A handbag and scarf was also named in lawsuit. The lawyer representing Hells Angels claimed "This isn't just about money, it's about membership. If you've got one of these rings on, a member might get really upset that you're an impostor." Saks refused to comment, Zappos had no immediate comment and the company's parent company, PPR, could not be reached for comment. The company settled the case with the Hells Angels after agreeing to remove all of the merchandise featuring the logo from sale on their website, stores and concessions and recalling any of the goods which have already been sold and destroying them.

In Fall 2012, in the United States District Court for the Eastern District of California, Hells Angels sued Toys "R" Us for trademark infringement, unfair competition, and dilution in relation to the sale of yo-yos manufactured by Yomega Corporation, a co-defendant, which allegedly bear the "Death Head" logo. In its complaint, Hells Angels asserted that the mark used on the yo-yos is likely to confuse the public into mistakenly believing that the toys originate with Hells Angels and Yomega filed counterclaims against Hells Angels for cancellation of the "Death Head" registrations on grounds of alleged fraud in the procurement of the registrations. The case settled and the lawsuit was dismissed with prejudice.

As of December 2013, the Hell's Angels sells its branded merchandise at a retail store in Toronto, Canada. Over seven years, it has defended its brand and label against use in clothes, jewelry, posters, and yo-yos.

Membership

A club member at a biker gathering
in Australia, 2008.

In order to become a Hells Angels prospect, candidates
must have a valid driver's license, a motorcycle over 750cc
and have the right combination of personal qualities. It is
said the club excludes child molesters and individuals who
have applied to become police or prison officers.

After a lengthy, phased process, a prospective member is
first deemed to be a "hang-around", indicating that the
individual is invited to some club events or to meet club
members at known gathering places.

If the hang-around is interested, he may be asked to
become an "associate", a status that usually lasts a year or
two. At the end of that stage, he is reclassified as
"prospect", participating in some club activities, but not

having voting privileges while he is evaluated for suitability as a full member. The last phase, and highest membership status, is "Full Membership" or "Full-Patch". The term "Full-Patch" refers to the complete four-piece crest, including the "Death Head" logo, two rockers (top rocker: "Hells Angels"; bottom rocker: state or territory claimed) and the rectangular "MC" patch below the wing of the Death's Head. Prospects are allowed to wear only a bottom rocker with the state or territory name along with the rectangular "MC" patch.

Hells Angels clubhouse in Oakland, California

To become a full member, the prospect must be voted on unanimously by the rest of the full club members. Prior to votes being cast, a prospect usually travels to every chapter in the sponsoring chapter's geographic jurisdiction (state/province/territory) and introduces himself to every Full-Patch member. This process allows each voting member to become familiar with the subject and to ask any questions of concern prior to the vote. Some form of formal induction follows, wherein the prospect affirms his loyalty to the club and its members. The final logo patch (top "Hells Angels" rocker) is then awarded at this initiation ceremony. The step of attaining full membership can be referred to as "being patched".

Even after a member is patched-in, the patches themselves remain the property of HAMC rather than the member. On leaving the Hells Angels, or being ejected, they must be returned to the club.

Worldwide chapters

The Hells Angels clubhouse at 77 East 3rd Street between First and Second Avenues in
the East Village neighborhood of Manhattan, New York City

The HAMC acknowledges more than one hundred chapters spread over 29 countries. Europe did not become widely home to the Hells Angels until 1969 when two London chapters were formed. The Beatles' George Harrison invited some members of the HAMC San Francisco to stay at Apple Records in London in 1968. According to Chris O'Dell, only two members showed up at Apple Records, Frisco Pete and Bill "Sweet William" Fritsch. Two people from London visited California, "prospected", and ultimately joined. Two charters were issued on July 30, 1969; one for "South London" - the re-imagined chapter renewing the already existing 1950 South London chapter - and the other for "East London", but by 1973 the two charters came together as one, simply called "London". The London Angels provided security at a number of UK Underground festivals including Phun City in 1970 organized by anarchist, *International Times* writer and lead singer with The Deviants, Mick Farren. They even awarded Farren an "approval patch" in 1970 for use on his first solo album *Mona*, which also featured Steve Peregrin Took (who was credited as "Shagrat the Vagrant"). The 1980s and 1990s saw a major expansion of the club into Canada.

A list of acknowledged chapters can be found on the HAMC's official website.

Racial policies

The club claims not to be a racially segregated organization, although at least one chapter allegedly requires that a candidate be a white male, and Sonny Barger stated in a BBC interview in 2000 that "The club, as a whole, is not racist but we probably have enough racist members that no black guy is going to get in it". At that time the club had no black members.

However there have been black members of puppet clubs, notably Gregory Wooley, a high-ranking member of the Rockers MC in Montreal who was the protégé and bodyguard of Hells Angel boss Maurice Boucher (who had been labeled a white supremacist by the media). Wooley became an associate of the Hells Angels Montreal chapter in the 1990s and later tried uniting street gangs in Quebec after Boucher was imprisoned.

In another interview with leader Sonny Barger in 2000 he remarked "if you're a motorcycle rider and you're white, you want to join the Hell's Angels. If you [*sic*] black, you want to join the Dragons. That's how it is whether anyone likes it or not. We don't have no blacks and they don't have no whites." When asked if that could change Sonny replied "Anything can change, I can't predict the future". Tobie Levingston who formed the black motorcycle club East Bay Dragons MC wrote in his book that he and Sonny Barger have a long-lasting friendship and that the Hells Angels and Dragons have a mutual friendship and hang out and ride together.

In a 1966 article about motorcycle rebels in the African-American community magazine *Ebony*, the Chosen Few MC stated that they see no racial animosity in the Hells Angels and that when they come into Chosen Few territory they all get together and just party. A Hells Angel member interviewed for the magazine insisted there was no racial prejudice in any of their clubs and stated "we don't have any negro members" but maintained there have not been any blacks who have sought membership. At one point in the 1970s the Hells Angels were looking to consolidate the different motorcycle clubs and offered every member of the Chosen Few MC a Hells Angel badge, but the Chosen Few turned down the offer.

Hell's Lovers

Hell's Lovers MC

Founded: 1967
Location: Chicago, Illinois
Founder: Frank "Claim-Jumper" Rios
Type: Outlaw motorcycle club
Region: Alabama, Colorado, Georgia, Illinois, Maryland, Tennessee and Texas
Membership: 1,500

Hell's Lovers is a multi-ethnic outlaw motorcycle club founded in Chicago in 1967, currently with about 1,500 members in the US. One of the first integrated biker clubs in Chicago, the club was founded by Frank "Claim-Jumper" Rios after he was denied membership in another motorcycle club. The club's motto is, "Death is my sidekick and the highway is my home."

In June 2008, the Ironhorse Roundup Bike Show, a swap meet at the Lake County Fairgrounds, was canceled by Grayslake, Illinois mayor Timothy Perry after state and Federal law enforcement authorities had warned the Grayslake police chief of threats of violence between the Hell's Lovers and a rival outlaw gang, the Outlaws Motorcycle Club.

The Wisconsin Department of Justice describes criminal activity by the Hell's Lovers as "decreasing," but says they have been associated with cocaine trafficking and motorcycle theft.

Highwaymen Motorcycle Club

Highwaymen MC

Motto: Highwaymen forever, forever Highwaymen
Founded: 1954
Location: Detroit, Michigan
Type: Outlaw motorcycle club
Region: Midwestern and Southern United States
Website: www.detroithighwaymen.com

The **Highwaymen Motorcycle Club** is a one-percenter outlaw motorcycle gang that was formed in Detroit, Michigan in 1954. The club has undergone a number of large-scale police and FBI investigations, most notably in 1973, 1987 and 2007.[2] In the early 1970s several members were convicted of bombings and raids of the homes and the clubhouses of rival motorcycle clubs.

The club is the largest in the Detroit area, with over one hundred members, and chapters in Alabama, Florida,

Indiana, Kentucky, Ohio, and Tennessee. Their insignia is a winged skeleton wearing a motorcycle cap and leather jacket, and their colors are black and silver. The club's motto is "*Highwaymen forever, forever Highwaymen*" ("*H.F.F.H.*"). James Blake Miller, the "Marlboro Marine", is a member of the Kentucky Highwaymen, many of whom, like Miller, are veterans suffering from posttraumatic stress disorder. The Highwaymen are banned from the Detroit Federation of Motorcycle Clubs, which was created by the president of the Detroit Outlaws Motorcycle Club in the 1970s to resolve motorcycle gang turf wars.

In 1955, the Highwaymen were actually listed as an American Motorcyclist Association (AMA) sanctioned club, a form of mainstream respectability which outlaw motorcycle clubs would, over the course of the 1950s and 1960s, come to reject as the very definition of 'outlaw' and 'one-percenter,' just as much as the AMA rejected outlaw clubs from their midst.

Criminal activities

Detroit Highwaymen clubhouse, the best-maintained building in the neighborhood. It was subject to forfeiture in 2010 for being a drug den.

On May 5, 2007, the Federal Bureau of Investigation arrested 40 members and associates of the Detroit chapter of the Highwaymen on a number of charges including racketeering, murder for hire, assault, police corruption, cocaine trafficking, vehicle theft, and mortgage and insurance fraud. Twenty-nine illegal firearms, including assault rifles, shotguns and handguns, were also found when FBI agents raided homes and the chapter's clubhouse. The investigation into the club lasted two years and involved wiretaps and two informants, one of whom was eventually murdered.

High-ranking Highwaymen member Randell Lee McDaniel was arrested for running a chop shop in Lansing, Michigan on June 13, 2007. The investigation by the Monroe County Auto Theft Enforcement began in October 2006 and served several search warrants on properties owned by McDaniel. He was charged with conducting a criminal enterprise, operating a chop shop, motor vehicle theft and possessing a controlled substance.

Four police officers and a member of the Highwaymen were indicted on March 12, 2008 by a federal grand jury in Detroit on charges stemming from the 2007 investigation into drug trafficking. Highwaymen member Sean Donovan, who was already incarcerated on stolen property charges, was charged with possession with intent to distribute marijuana and Vicodin. The four police officers were also jailed for corruption.

Iron Horsemen

Iron Horsemen MC

Motto: Ashes to ashes, dust to dust, if it weren't for the Iron Horsemen, the highways would rust
Founded: Mid-1960s
Type: Outlaw motorcycle club
Region: Northeastern and Midwestern United States
Website: www.ironhorsemenmc.com

The **Iron Horsemen Motorcycle Club** is an outlaw motorcycle club that was founded in Cincinnati, Ohio in the mid-1960s. The word 'outlaw' itself carries a specific meaning which does not imply immediate criminal intent; rather it means the club is not sanctioned by the American Motorcyclist Association (AMA) and does not adhere to the AMA's rules. The club now also has chapters in Kansas, Pennsylvania, Tennessee, Indiana, California, Kentucky, Maine, New Jersey, Massachusetts, Maryland, and New York. Their insignia is a winged, metallic horse's head and their motto is "*Ashes to ashes, dust to dust, if it weren't for the Iron Horsemen, the highways would rust*". Law enforcement classifies them as an "Outlaw Motorcycle Gang".

Iron Horsemen MC (Australia)

There is also another motorcycle club in Australia, founded in Melbourne during 1969, which uses the same name.

Publicized crimes

Police arrested three Iron Horsemen for beating an off duty police officer to death and assaulting another on April 20, 1997. The attacks took place on two different occasions at bars in Hollywood, Maryland.

Two members of the Iron Horsemen were sentenced to five years in prison, and another three were given sixteen years in total on June 26, 2008 for drug dealing. They sold methamphetamine and speed in the Western District of Kentucky between December 2003 and December 2005, and distributed between 50 and 200 grams each. Both the Drug Enforcement Administration (DEA) and the Bureau of Alcohol, Tobacco, Firearms and Explosives (ATF) were involved in the case.

On May 19, 2009, 15 Iron Horsemen, including a State President, were convicted of drug trafficking at the District Court in Portland, Maine. They smuggled cocaine and marijuana, which they obtained from drug cartels in Mexico, to Atlanta, Georgia and then Haverhill, Massachusetts before trafficking it to Maine where they distributed it throughout the state. The ring operated from 2004 until December 2007. The DEA and ATF investigated the club for over a year and carried out the final raids on March 12, 2008. During these raids, they arrested a total of 29 people and seized 10 kilos of cocaine, 600 pounds of marijuana, AK-47s, AR-15s, handguns and $37,000 in cash. The case was known as "Operation Trojan Horse".

One member of the Iron Horsemen was shot in a gunfight with Cincinnati Police on September 18, 2010. Local media reported that a gang member opened fire on several identifiable police officers and 2 undercover officers as they approached JD's Honky Tonk and Emporium escorted by marked police cruisers. The two undercover officers were injured and the gunman that started the incident was killed in the shooting.

Many other reports say that one member of the Iron Horsemen was arrested in New York for possession of firearms and cocaine. This man was known as Big Ed.

In 2013, four members of the Iron Horsemen were arrested in Rochester, New York. William Heinrich, Dustin Harper, David Orbaker and Douglas Tallent were charged with Gang Assault in the second degree, a class C felony in New York State. Police say the four men seriously injured a 40-year-old man at a bar on South Avenue in Rochester.

Lone Legion Brotherhood

Lone Legion Brotherhood

Type: Outlaw motorcycle club
Region: USA, New Zealand
Abbreviation: LLBMA

The **Lone Legion Motorcycle Association** is an outlaw motorcycle club which started in the USA and now has chapters located in New Zealand.

According to media and Police the club is a member of the "A-Team", an alliance between several NZ biker groups including the Outcasts MC, the Epitaph Riders MC, the

Forty-Fives MC, the Southern Vikings MC, Satan's Slaves MC, Sinn Fein MC and the Lost Breed MC.

Market Street Commandos

The **Market Street Commandos** was a motorcycle club that, in 1947, along with the Boozefighters and the Pissed Off Bastards of Bloomington, participated in the highly publicized Hollister incident (later immortalized on film as *The Wild One*). In 1954 the Fontana Hells Angels merged with the Market Street Commandos to become the San Francisco chapter of the Hells Angels.

Mongols Motorcycle Club

Mongols Motorcycle Club

Founded: 1969
Location: East Los Angeles, California
Key people: Primarily Hispanic American and Native American (in the USA)
Primarily Mhallami in Germany
Type: Outlaw motorcycle club
Region: USA, Europe, Mexico, Israel, Australia
Membership: 1000-1500
Website: www.mongolsmc.com

The **Mongols Motorcycle Club**, sometimes called the **Mongol Nation** or **Mongol Brotherhood**, is a "one-percenter" outlaw motorcycle club and alleged organized crime syndicate. The club is headquartered in southern California and was originally formed in Montebello, California, in 1969. Law enforcement officials estimate there are approximately 1000-1500 full-patched members (with the expansion in Australia in 2013). The Mongols' main presence is in southern California, with chapters in 14 states, as well as international chapters in 13 countries.

Criminal activities

The Mongols members have had long-running confrontations with law enforcement in such areas as drug dealing (especially methamphetamine), money laundering, robbery, extortion, firearms violations, murder, and assault, among other crimes.

Incidents

In 1998, ATF agent William Queen infiltrated the club, eventually becoming a full-patch member and rising to the rank of treasurer using the undercover alias of Billy St. John. In April 2000, based on evidence gathered during Queen's 28-month undercover time with the club, 54 Mongols were arrested. All but one of the accused were later convicted of various crimes including drug trafficking, motorcycle theft, and conspiracy to commit murder.

In 2002, members of the Mongols and the Hells Angels had a confrontation in Laughlin, Nevada, at the Harrah's Laughlin Casino, that left three bikers dead.[1] Mongol Anthony 'Bronson' Barrera, 43, was stabbed to death; and two Hells Angels — Jeramie Bell, 27, and Robert Tumelty, 50, — were shot to death. On February 23, 2007, Hells Angels members James Hannigan and Rodney Cox were sentenced to two years in prison for their respective roles in the incident. Cox and Hannigan were captured on videotape confronting Mongols inside the casino. A Hells Angels member can be clearly seen on the casino security videotape performing a front kick on a Mongol which in turn started the ensuing melee.

Mongols member Christopher Ablett turned himself in to authorities in Bartlesville, Oklahoma, on October 4, 2008 after going on the run for murdering Hells Angels President Mark "Papa" Guardado in San Francisco, California earlier that year. The San Francisco Police Department had issued a $5 million arrest warrant for him. He was convicted of murder in aid of racketeering and three gun charges on February 23, 2012, in San Francisco.

On December 20, 2008, in Las Vegas, Mongols members arrived at "A Special Memories Wedding Chapel" for a fellow member's wedding, to find a local Hells Angels charter were just finishing up their own ceremony. It is reported by KTNV Channel 13 news, that the Hells Angels attacked the Mongols members, sending three to a hospital, two of whom suffered from stab wounds. No arrests were made and local authorities report that they are looking for suspects said to be involved in the attack.

Operation Black Rain

Operation Black Rain was an operation by the ATF in 2008 to stop alleged criminal activity within the Mongols Motorcycle Club.

On October 21, 2008, 38 members, including Ruben "Doc" Cavazos, were taken into Federal custody after four Bureau of Alcohol, Tobacco, Firearms and Explosives agents infiltrated the group for a second time, becoming full patch members. 110 arrest warrants and 160 search warrants were issued in California, Ohio, Colorado, Nevada, Washington, and Oregon. On October 23, 2008, US District Court Judge Florence-Marie Cooper granted an injunction that prohibits club members, their family members and associates from wearing, licensing, selling, or distributing the logo, which typically depicts the profile of a Mongolian warrior wearing sunglasses, because according to the police, they use the logo and names as an identity and as a form of intimidation to fulfill their goals. Prosecutors requested the injunction after authorities arrested dozens of Mongols under a racketeering indictment.

The club president Ruben Cavazos and others pleaded guilty to the racketeering charge and Cavazos faces up to 20 years in prison along with the others arrested. Cavazos was later voted out of the club by its members on August 30, 2008.

A planned weekend meeting in Lancaster, California, expected to draw 800 Mongols and their families, was blocked after city officials shut down and fenced off the hotel they had booked for the event, which coincides with the "Celebrate Downtown Lancaster" festival. The mayor had previously threatened to shut down the hotel over unpaid taxes if the agreement to host the Mongols was not canceled. An attorney for the Mongols said he plans to sue the city and the mayor, potentially for civil rights violations, after previously threatening to sue the hotel for breach of contract should they comply with the mayor's demands. Mayor R. Rex Parris said he wants to keep the Mongols out because they "are engaged in domestic terrorism...and they kill our children."

After a long legal battle with the DOJ and ATF over the Mongols' MC patch, the Mongols won the rights to continued use and ownership of their patch.

The television show *America's Most Wanted* had exclusive access to the operation, and broadcast, behind-the-scenes footage of the many arrests.

Mongols MC Germany

A German chapter of Mongols MC was founded in Bremen by members of the local crime syndicate run by Lebanese immigrants in 2010. It was the first time that a Muslim clan-based crime syndicate in Germany became active in the field of outlaw motorcycle clubs. Organized crime in Bremen is dominated by the Miri-Clan, a large family of Lebanese origin with an estimated 2,600 members, who first migrated to Germany beginning in the late 1980s, and rose to national notoriety with a number of large-scale criminal activities in 2010.

According to Andreas Weber, the state of Bremen's chief of criminal investigation, the new Mongols chapter is only nominally a motorcycle group. Clan members do not have motorcycle licences and drive around the city in cars. Presumably, they are interested in associating themselves with the US motorcycle club primarily to profit from their infrastructure and trading channels in drug trafficking. The president of Mongols Bremen, "Mustafa B." accidentally killed himself with his bike as a novice licence holder briefly after the chapter's foundation. He was presumably succeeded by "Ibrahim M.", who is on record with 147 felonies ranging from grievous bodily harm to illegal possession of a weapon.

Local daily newspaper Kölnische Rundschau reports that a further German Mongols chapter has become active in Cologne, which is a traditional Hells Angels area.

Mongols MC Michigan

During the 1970s and 1980s there was a Mongols Motorcycle Club based out of Michigan with other chapters in Ohio, Pennsylvania, and Delaware. The Mongols MC based out of Michigan were not affiliated with the Mongols MC from southern California. Chapters of the Michigan based Mongols MC have since been dissolved or absorbed into larger motorcycle clubs like the Outlaws MC.

Mongols MC Australia

In October 2013 the Finks MC had a national meeting in Adelaide and voted to patch over the Mongols MC. The move makes the Mongols one of the largest bike gangs in Australia with 400 members. The patch over was attributed to a need to change the culture, to move from a gang back to a motorcycle club and institute a structure whereby there were consequences for actions. Police dismissed the reasons given for the patch over as propaganda.

Mongols Alcohol, Drugs and Criminal Conviction Policy

1. Any member using, selling, transporting or possession heroin, cocaine or any other illegal drug which includes marijuana shall be automatically expelled from the club.

2. Any members convicted of any serious felony including, but not limited to, murder, rape, robbery, or burglary shall be automatically expelled from the club as soon as the conviction is final.

3. No member shall inject or be injected with any illegal drug or face automatic expulsion from the club; the only exception is a valid and proven legal medication.

4. Officers in charge at a club function shall maintain a high degree of sobriety or face disciplinary action.

5. No member shall smoke cocaine or speed. Violations will result in expulsion from the club.

6. If a Brother with a drug problem comes to the club and asks for help, rather than getting caught, an exception can be made depending on the circumstances.

7. The club is not responsible for lawyers or bail bondsmen unless a national officer has authorised it.

8. If a member knowingly acts out on his own and is arrested for guns, drugs or any illegal activity, it is not the responsibility of the club to provide a lawyer or a bail bondsman for his actions.

Notorious (motorcycle club)

Notorious MC

Founded: 2007
Founding location: Sydney, New South Wales, Australia
Years active: 2007-2012
Territory: Sydney
Ethnicity: Middle Eastern and Pacific Islanders
Membership: Unknown
Criminal activities: Drug trafficking, arms dealing, extortion, prostitution, money laundering, Drive-by shootings, Armed robbery, Murder, assault, Kidnapping
Allies: Parra Boyz (Asesinoz MC)
Rivals; Bandidos, Comancheros and Hells Angels

Notorious is a former gang that was based in Sydney, Australia. They claimed to be an outlaw motorcycle club; however, not all members ride motorcycles. Its emblem features a skull with a turban brandishing twin pistols and the words "Original Gangster" beneath it, along with the motto "Only the dead see the end of war". Labeled as one of Australia's most dangerous gangs, they had been feuding with larger and well-known motorcycle gangs including the Hells Angels and the Bandidos. As of March 2012 the gang no longer exists as an organized structure after being dismantled by a police operation arresting key members and with other members choosing to quit the gang life.

Overview

Creation

Established in 2007, Notorious was formed by senior members and associates of the Nomads motorcycle gang, after the Parramatta Nomads branch was disbanded. The newly formed gang, founded by Alan Sarkis, then started to recruit youth of Middle Eastern background and aligned itself with street gangs to boost its numbers to gain supremacy over rival gangs.

Members

The exact number of Notorious members is unknown to police but sources claim the gang has up to 200 active members. Its members are sometimes called "Nike bikies", for wearing expensive nike running shoes (nike air max & nike tns usually the footwear of choice), fashionable t-shirts and being clean shaven, in contrast to the traditional bikie image of dirty jackets, leather boots and beards.

Police have named John Ibrahim, a celebrity Nightclub entrepreneur and his three brothers Sam, Fadi and Michael Ibrahim as senior members of Notorious.[8] Allan Sarkis has been named as the president of Notorious but Police believe Sam Ibrahim formed the gang and is the driving force behind it, Ibrahim denies creating Notorious but admits knowing its members.

Involvement In crime

President of Notorious Allan Sarkis denies his club being involved in organized crime and denies any knowledge of a feud with other gangs, He claims the club has a very strict policy on drugs, even though Notorious members as young as 14 have been charged with possession and drugs supply. In an exclusive interview with The Sydney Morning Herald, Sarkis stated:

> "Linking us to drugs, or the drug trade, is way out of line. We want to be acknowledged and respected as a motorcycle club, not as gangsters."

Timeline

- March 2007, Rugby League stars Jarryd Hayne and Mark Gasnier were involved in a violent brawl with Notorious members at Sydney's Kings Cross, where a Notorious member ended up firing a number of shots toward the football stars. It was later revealed that the incident was Notorious's "coming-out party", the first time the new gang appeared on police radar.
- October 2008, Allan Sarkis escaped death after a bomb exploded under his luxury car. The $90,000

car was parked under his exclusive Lane Cove apartment complex. It is believed the Comancheros were behind the bombing.

- On 5 October 2008, senior Notorious member Todd O'Connor was executed in a back street in the Sydney suburb of Tempe. *The Sydney Morning Herald* reported that Notorious is believed to be involved in a dispute with other outlaw motorcycle groups for control of the drug trade in Kings Cross and Oxford Street.
- October 2008, champion kickboxer Mustafa Assoum who volunteered at a Muslim youth centre was executed next to a phone box he was using, Notorious have been linked to the shooting.
- January, 2009, Notorious is suspected of being behind the shooting of a tattoo parlour and bombing of a Hells Angels clubhouse.
- February 2009, several Notorious members wearing balaclavas entered a clubhouse and shot three members of the Nomads motorcycle gang.
- 20 March 2009, relatives of Notorious members were the targets of several drive-by shootings across Sydney. The Bandidos are suspected of being behind the Shooting.
- 22 March 2009, a wild shootout between Notorious and Banditos members took place in a Sydney street, involving six homes in three streets, leaving two men aged 18 and 17 in hospital.
- 29 March 2009, an un-exploded bomb was placed by Notorious members at the family home of a senior Bandidos member – police received a tip-off from the public and the Bomb Squad rushed to the scene but the Bandido member and his family refused to leave their home.
- June 2009, Fadi Ibrahim, brother of John Ibrahim and a member of Notorious, survived a murder

attempt. He was shot five times while sitting in his Lamborghini parked outside his Castle Cove mansion.

- September 2009, Fadi Ibrahim and younger brother Michael were charged after a plot to murder bikie associate John Macris was uncovered by detectives.
- May 2010 - Jihad Murad, a senior member of Notorious and his girlfriend came under attack after a car pulled up next to them at a street light and fired 12 shots into their car. Those in the vehicle survived but police believe the Comancheros, who are involved in a violent feud with Notorious were responsible for the attack.
- August 2010, Hameed Ullah Dastagir was charged with attempted murder for allegedly stabbing 21-year old Giovanni Focarelli in the stomach and chest outside his father's Hindley Street tattoo parlour in Adelaide, South Australia. Dastagir was wearing a Notorious jumper during the attack and witnesses claim hearing Focarelli say "Notorious got me" while stumbling back into his father's tattoo parlour.
- October 2010 - president Allan Sarkis and another senior member of Notorious were charged by police after attacking two members of the Comanchero Motorcycle Club at a cafe in Bondi. One of the Commancheros had his ankle broken by one of the Notorious members during the attack.
- November 2010, Armani Stelio - the sister of the Ibrahim brothers had her family home peppered with bullets. More than 20 shots were fired into her home and nearby cars. Lawyers for the Ibrahim family claim they were "wrongly targeted", although investigators fear revenge attacks.
- November 2010, just hours after the drive-by shooting of Armani Stelio's family home, Saber

Murad, a member of Notorious was gunned down outside his home. In a statement, police revealed *There are links between the Notorious crime gang and both locations.*

- December 2010, "Coogee Ink", a tattoo parlour owned by senior Commancheros was firebombed with Notorious being the prime suspects. The parlour is owned by Comanchero national president Daux Ngakuru and his right-hand man Mark Buddle. *The Daily Telegraph* revealed Mark Buddle, 32, was attacked by Notorious members outside a Bondi cafe in October 2010.
- 13 January 2011, oldest brother Sam Ibrahim was shot in the legs in a drive-by outside his parents' home in Merrylands in Sydney's south west.

Outlaws Motorcycle Club

Outlaws Motorcycle Club

Motto: God Forgives, Outlaws Don't.
ADIOS (Angels Die In Outlaw States)
Founded: 1935
Location: McCook, Illinois, United States
Type: Outlaw motorcycle club
Region: Worldwide
Marque: American-made motorcycles
Website: www.outlawsmcworld.com
Abbreviation: AOA

The **Outlaws Motorcycle Club**, incorporated as the **American Outlaws Association** or its acronym, **A.O.A.**, is a one-percenter motorcycle club that was formed in McCook, Illinois in 1935.

Membership in the Outlaws is limited to men who own American-made motorcycles of a particular size, although in Europe motorcycles from any country are allowed so long as they are in the chopper style. Their main rivals are the Hells Angels, giving rise to a phrase used by Outlaws members, "ADIOS" (the Spanish word for "goodbye", but in this case doubling as an acronym for "**A**ngels **D**ie **I**n **O**utlaw **S**tates").

History

The Outlaws Motorcycle Club was established out of Matilda's Bar on old Route 66 in McCook, Illinois, a southwestern suburb of Chicago, in 1935. The club stayed together during World War II, but like most organizations at that time, their activities were limited.

In the 1950s, the club's logo was changed; a small skull replaced a winged motorcycle, and Old English-style letters were adopted. This design was embroidered on a black shirt and hand painted on leather jackets. In 1954, the Crossed Pistons were added to the original small skull. This design was embroidered on a black western-style shirt with white piping. The movie *The Wild One* with Marlon Brando influenced this backpatch. The Skull and Crossed Pistons were redesigned in 1959, making them much larger with more detail. The A.O.A. logo was adopted as an answer to the A.M.A. logo.

The Outlaws became an official member of the 1%er Brotherhood of Clubs in 1963.

The club featured in a work of photojournalism called *The Bikeriders* published in 1967 by Danny Lyon, a collection of photographs and interviews documenting the lifestyle of members of the club in the early 1960s.

In England and Wales the group has around 30 different chapters.

Clubs with similar names

A number of one percenter motorcycle clubs are called the "Outlaws", e.g. New Zealand. These are not part of the AOA and share only the name, having a different patch design and colors. In some countries, independent Outlaw MCs have joined, or been "patched over" to the now worldwide club.

Criminal cases

United States

Florida

The FBI's Ten Most Wanted Fugitive#453, Taco Bowman, known World Leader of the AOA, in prison since 1999 for three murders, was the international president of the Outlaws Motorcycle Club. During the time that Bowman was a fugitive in 1998, it had chapters in more than 30 cities in the United States and some 20 chapters in at least four other countries. In 2001 he was tried in Jacksonville, Florida. Federal agents along with the Daytona Beach SWAT Team raided the Outlaws clubhouse on Beach Street in Daytona Beach, Florida looking for drugs, weapons, contraband, paraphernalia, etc.; they tore the Daytona Beach clubhouse apart for the better part of the day and found nothing, but removed as many of the club's pictures and any other possibly identifying information as they could find. Federal agents also raided a home in Ormond Beach and two other clubhouses around the state. The search of the Jacksonville clubhouses netted federal agents 60 weapons including pocket and kitchen knives. U.S. Attorney General Alberto Gonzales announced a Detroit grand jury indictment of 16 of the Outlaws National

Club's members. The Detroit grand jury indictment included various charges, including assault and drug distribution. Eleven Outlaws leaders and high-ranking members of the gang were arrested after a five-year investigation. The FBI said several gang members were charged with conspiracy to commit assault on members of the Hells Angels Motorcycle Club in Indiana.

Georgia

Frank Rego Vital of Roberta, Georgia, an Outlaws MC member, was shot and killed in an early morning gunfight June 24, 2007 in the parking lot of The Crazy Horse Saloon strip club in Forest Park, Georgia by two members of the Renegades MC in what has been described as a self-defense shooting after Vital and other Outlaws members followed the men from the club. Both Renegade members were shot several times but survived.

Illinois

On July 30, 2008, several facilities associated with the Outlaws in the Chicago area were raided by agents from the FBI and the ATF. The FBI brought in a SWAT team and an urban assault vehicle to the clubhouse in the west side of the city in case violence were to break out.

Indiana

On July 11, 2012, U.S. Marshalls raided the Indianapolis Outlaws Chapter clubhouse and arrested 42 members for crimes ranging from mail fraud to money laundering. Law enforcement agencies conducted the raids at dawn in an attempt to catch members off guard. U.S. Attorney Joe Hogsett said their offenses included using violence to collect debts and illegal gambling operations.

Maine

On June 15, 2010 the ATF surrounded the home of Thomas "Tomcat" Mayne. Gunfire was exchanged with the ATF, ultimately killing Mayne. The ATF was there to serve a federal search warrant for an indictment that included Mayne and 26 other members of the Outlaws, for RICO charges and for the shooting of a member of the rival Hells Angels.

New Hampshire

On June 27, 2006 Christopher Legere of Raymond, New Hampshire, an Outlaws member, was arrested in the murder of a man who was wearing a Hells Angels shirt. The victim, John Denoncourt, 32, of Manchester, New Hampshire, was shot and killed outside the 3-Cousins Pizza and Lounge in Manchester on Sunday June 25, 2006 after he was spotted hugging the bartender, who was Legere's girlfriend. Denoncourt, according to friends and family, was not a Hells Angel member himself but had friends who were. Legere had been involved in another incident in Connecticut in early 2006 when he was charged with illegal possession of body armor by a convicted felon.

Pennsylvania

On March 17, 2009, 22 people—including a correctional officer—were charged in connection with a $3.6 million cocaine distribution ring operated by members and "wannabes" of the Outlaws Motorcycle Club in Luzerne County, Pennsylvania.

On August 24, 2009, 15 members of the Outlaws Philadelphia chapter were arrested in connection with a methamphetamine ring. Those arrested included chapter president Thomas "The Boss" Zaroff, Jr., and Charles "The Panhead" Rees. According to Pennsylvania District Attorney Tom Corbett, the gang sold methamphetamine in Philadelphia, Bucks, Montgomery, Chester, and Delaware counties in Pennsylvania and in Camden and Burlington counties in New Jersey.

Tennessee

On January 1, 2010, the Knox County Sheriff's Office in conjunction with the Knoxville Police Department raided a house located at 205 Clifton Road to serve two arrest warrants and execute a search warrant on the property alleged to be an Outlaw clubhouse. Officers, including members of the SWAT team, raided the facility just before midnight but found only a handful of elderly club members, who surrendered quickly and peaceably. Knox County Sheriff James Jones acted on information from an undercover informant that many of the members of the club would be present at the informal celebration of New Year's Eve. Arrest warrants had been issued for Mark "Ivan" Lester and Kenneth Foster for their alleged roles in a confrontation with the undercover informant earlier in December 2009, who had infiltrated the organization over 14 months ago. According to Sheriff Jones, Lester and Foster allegedly threatened the informant with a pistol and demanded the colors in his possession. By Club bylaws Club colors always remain the property of the Club and not of the individual member. The informant, who claimed to be in fear of their safety, submitted to the men's demands. Mark Lester is alleged to be the Regional President in charge of the clubs operations in the states of Kentucky and Tennessee. Kenneth Foster is alleged to be the local Knoxville chapter Outlaw Motorcycle Club President.

Both Lester and Foster were arrested at the residence and were charged with aggravated robbery and aggravated kidnapping. Upon search of the residence the officers found a few legally owned handguns and small amounts of marijuana. They alleged they had evidence of other illegal activities. Both men were jailed and held in lieu of 3 million dollar bonds. Other than the charges stemming from the club's unmasking of the undercover officer, however, no other charges have been filed.

Virginia

On June 15, 2010, a grand jury in Virginia indicted 27 Outlaws members on various charges under the Racketeer Influenced and Corrupt Organizations Act (RICO) related to participating in a criminal enterprise that engaged in assaults, kidnapping, drug dealing, illegal gambling, and attempted murder.

United Kingdom

On August 12, 2007, Hells Angel Gerry Tobin, a Canadian living in Mottingham, London, was shot dead on the M40 motorway while returning from the Bulldog Bash festival held near Long Marston, Warwickshire. He was singled out at random by members of the Outlaws. In November 2008, seven members of the Warwickshire chapter, were convicted of his murder and sentenced to life imprisonment.

On January 20, 2008, there was a brawl between up to 30 of the rival clubs at Birmingham International Airport. Police recovered various weapons including knuckledusters, hammers and a meat cleaver. Four Outlaw members and three Hells Angels were imprisoned for six years each. Increased security at the court, for the period of the trial, cost around £1 million.

Belgium

In April 2000 full-patch member Jan Wouters was killed by Outlaw André Renard in the presence of two other Outlaws on the club's domain in Mechelen. All three members were given life sentences for the murder of their fellow Outlaw. Among them was the brother-in-law of the victim. According to the three convicted Outlaws the murder took place after an argument escalated. Upon escalation Wouters supposedly aimed a gun at his brother-in-law after which he himself was killed. It was largely believed that the murder was not the result of an escalated discussion, but rather an execution approved by the club's hierarchy.

On October 4, 2009 several Hells Angels and allied Red Devils performed a raid on an Outlaw MC clubhouse in Kortrijk. Shots were fired and three Outlaws were wounded before the Hells Angels and their Red Devils comrades fled the scene. The incident occurred after members of the Outlaws MC supposedly pushed over a motorcycle belonging to Red Devils MC president Johan F. in Moeskroen. The raid is also thought to be a part of a territorial dispute between the Hells Angels and the Red Devils on one side and the Outlaws on the other. Several months before the raid, on the 24th of July 2009, members of the Red Devils and Hells Angels already retaliated by setting fire to motorcycles outside an Outlaw clubhouse. Eventually six Hells Angels and two Red Devils were convicted for attempted murder and given sentences from five to twenty years in prison.

On May 21, 2011 one full-patch member, one prospect, and one sympathizer of the Belgium Outlaws MC were shot and killed by rival bikers of the Belgian Hells Angels. The killings took place in Eisden, not far from Maasmechelen where the Outlaws had opened a new clubhouse just several days earlier. Two days after the murders several Hells Angels where linked to the murder and arrested, including the president of the 'Zwartberg' chapter. The funeral of the full-patch member, Freddy Put, was joined by some 200 Outlaws from across Europe. The investigation concerning the murders in Eisden is ongoing and is made difficult because within both the Hells Angels and the Outlaws there is a code of silence called 'omerta'. In a response to these murders the Belgian Army is investigating the possibility of removing members of criminal MC's from their ranks since two of the primary suspects were paracommandos.

In the night of 24 December 2012, during a rock concert in Dilsen-Stokkem, members of the Hells Angels were attacked by members of the Outlaws MC. Several Hells Angels were inside the *Nieuwenborgh* hall listening to the evening's last rock band finishing their final songs when, at about 1:30 a.m. by local time, several Outlaws armed with expandable batons (illegal in Belgium) arrived at the scene. The situation quickly escalated into a brawl with three wounded as a result. The police quickly arrived at the scene in large numbers. One of the wounded was a 41-year-old man who suffered an open fracture to the leg.

Pagan's Motorcycle Club

Pagan's MC

Founded 1959
Location Prince George's County, Maryland
Founder Lou Dobkin
Type Outlaw motorcycle club
Region East Coast of the United States

Pagan's Motorcycle Club, or simply **The Pagans**, is a one-percenter outlaw motorcycle gang and an alleged organized crime syndicate formed by Lou Dobkin in 1959 in Prince George's County, Maryland, United States. The club rapidly expanded and by 1965, the Pagans, originally clad in blue denim jackets and riding Triumphs, began to evolve along the lines of the stereotypical one percenter motorcycle club.

The Pagans are categorized as an outlaw motorcycle gang by the Federal Bureau of Investigation. They are known to fight over territory with the Hells Angels Motorcycle Club (HAMC) and other motorcycle clubs, such as Fates Assembly MC, who have since merged with the HAMC. It is active in thirteen states: Delaware, Florida, Kentucky, Maryland, New Jersey, New York, North Carolina, Ohio, Pennsylvania, South Carolina, Michigan, Virginia, and West Virginia.

Early history

The Pagans were established in Prince George County, Maryland by then president Lou Dobkin, in 1959. The group started out by wearing denim jackets and riding Triumph Motorcycles. Originally they were a comradeship of 13 motorcyclists. In the 1960s they adopted a formal constitution and formed a governing structure choosing a national president.

They were a fairly non-violent group until 1965, when the Pagans evolved into an outlaw biker gang with ties to other organized crime groups such as the American Mafia. Under the leadership of John "Satan" Marron their violence grew in the early 1970s. Their Mother Club is not in a fixed location but has been generally located in the North East.

Pagan leaders number 13 to 18 members who are chapter presidents with the largest chapter located in Philadelphia.

The Pagans have grown through merging with other smaller Outlaw Motorcycle gangs (OMG). Considered by law enforcement to be almost as complex and diversified as the Hells Angels, the discipline and structure of the Pagans is the most rigid of the Big Four OMGs.

Patch

The Pagans MC patch depicts the Norse fire-giant Surtr sitting on the sun, wielding a sword, plus the word *Pagan's* [sic] in red, white and blue. Unlike most one percenter motorcycle clubs, the Pagans do not include on their club insignia a bottom rocker indicating the geographical chapter of the member wearing the club's full patch. It is believed the club declines to follow this one percenter tradition because they do not want law enforcement to know what state chapters individual Pagans belong to.

Members wear blue denim vests called cuts or cutoffs with club patches, known as colors, on the front and back. Symbols of the Pagans also include a black number 13 on the back of their colors (indicating that they are affiliated with the club's Mother Chapter), the number "4" (which signifies the motto "live and die"), the number "5" (which signifies the Nazi SS motto), the number "7" (an "in memory of" patch) and the number "9" (the chapter with which the member is affiliated). Nazi or White supremacist patches are also common on the front of the cuts, as are tattoos reading "ARGO" (Ar Go Fuck Yourself) and "NUNYA" (Nun'Ya Fuckin' Business).

Membership

Recently, the Pagans' membership has begun to decline as their rival Hells Angels' membership has grown. Pagans have approximately 350 to 400 members and 44 chapters and are active along the East Coast of the United States. Chapters are common in Florida, New Jersey, Pennsylvania, Delaware, Maryland, North Carolina, Virginia and West Virginia. The Pagans have a Mother Club or ruling council which ultimately rules the gang. The Pagans headquarters is currently in Delaware County, Pennsylvania.

Members must be at least 21 years old and owners of Harley-Davidson motorcycles with engines 900 cc or larger. The national sergeant-at-arms' responsibility is to hand-pick 13 chapter members to serve as the "enforcers" or "regulators". This body uses violence and intimidation to prevent any and all opposition to the Mother Club.

Criminal activities

The Pagans have been linked to the production and smuggling of drugs such as methamphetamine, marijuana, cocaine, heroin, and PCP. The Pagans also have had strong ties to organized crime, especially in New Jersey and Pennsylvania. Pagans often use puppet clubs, smaller affiliated motorcycle clubs, or small street drug trafficking organizations that support larger Outlaw Motorcycle Gangs (OMGs) for distributing drugs. Pagans have also engaged in assault, arson, extortion, motorcycle/car theft, and weapons trafficking. Most of the violence carried out by the Pagans is directed to rival OMGs such as Hells Angels.

New Jersey

On July 17, 1994, at least eight members of the Pagans showed up at the annual charity picnic fund-raiser organized by Tri-County MC in Hackettstown, NJ. The Pagans were there to intimidate local motorcycle clubs into aligning with the Pagans so they would have a larger power base to prevent the Hell's Angels from getting established in New Jersey. A fight started and escalated from fist to knives and guns. When it was all done, Pagans Glenn Ritchie & Diego Vega had been shot dead. Pagan Ron Locke & Tri-County member William Johnson had gun shot wounds and Tri-County member Hank Riger had had his throat cut by Ron Locke.

New York/Pennsylvania

On February 23, 2002, 73 Pagans were arrested in Long Island, New York after appearing at an indoor motorcycle and tattoo expo called the Hellraiser Ball. The Pagans had shown up to the event to confront Hells Angels who were at the Ball. Dozens of Pagans rushed the doors of the event and were met with violence by the Hells Angels. Fighting ensued, ten people were wounded, and a Hells Angel allegedly shot and killed a Pagan member. Two weeks later, a Pagans owned tattoo parlor located in South Philadelphia, Pennsylvania was firebombed.

In 2005, Pagans allegedly opened fire on and killed the Vice-President of the Hells Angels' Philadelphia chapter as he was driving his truck on the Schuylkill Expressway.Later that year, the Hells Angels closed their Philadelphia chapter.

In September 2010, nineteen members of the Pagans were arrested in Rocky Point, New York for allegedly conspiring to murder members of the Hells Angels. Charges also include assault, distribution of cocaine and oxycodone, conspiracy to commit extortion and weapons charges. Two federal ATF agents, infiltrated the gang, providing key evidence. One agent eventually served as sergeant-at-arms, the second-highest position in the hierarchy. Gang members were heard plotting to murder members of the Hells Angels using homemade hand grenades.

Dennis Katona, alleged to be the club's "National President", was arrested by Pennsylvania State Police near Pittsburgh in Herminie in June 2011.

Maryland

A Pagans MC leader, Jay Carl Wagner, 66, was arrested in Washington County, Maryland, by 60 plus officers from state, local and federal officials with a bomb disposal robot on May 9, 2007, and later charged with possession of a regulated firearm after conviction of a violent crime. Police and agents recovered seven handguns, two alleged explosive devices and 13 long rifles. On March 5, 2008, Wagner pleaded guilty to being a felon in possession of a firearm. On August 8, 2008, U.S. District Chief Judge Benson E. Legg sentenced Wagner to 30 months in prison followed by three years of supervised release.

On 6 October 2009, the home of national president David "Bart" Barbeito in Myersville, Maryland was raided by police. He was arrested on firearms charges. In June, 2010 he pleaded guilty to racketeering and other charges. He was sentenced to thirty months confinement.

Multi-State

In 2009, 55 Pagans members and associates were arrested from West Virginia, Kentucky, Virginia, Pennsylvania, New York, New Jersey, Delaware and Florida. Charges range from attempted murder and kidnapping to drug dealing and conspiracy. So far, seven defendants in the case have pled guilty.

Pissed Off Bastards of Bloomington

Pissed Off Bastards of Bloomington

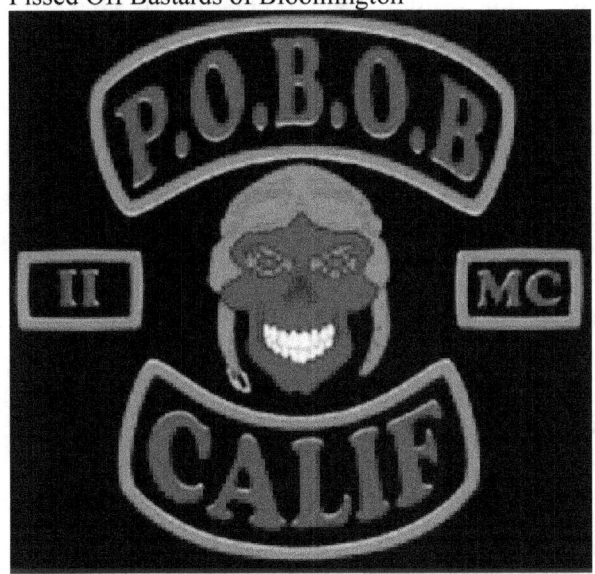

Motto: "The Original Wild Ones", "A drinking club with a motorcycle problem."
Founded: 1945
Type: Outlaw motorcycle club
Region: California and Nevada, USA
Activities: The original outlaw motorcycle and car club
Website: www.pobobmc.com

The **Pissed Off Bastards of Bloomington** (POBOB) is a motorcycle club that, in 1947, along with the Boozefighters and the Market Street Commandos, participated in the highly publicized Hollister riot (later immortalized on film as *The Wild One*).

After the Hollister incident, a prominent Pissed Off Bastard named Otto Friedli (28 Jun 1931 - 17 Mar 2008) split with the club and formed his own group on March 17, 1948 in Fontana, just west of San Bernardino. He called it the Hells Angels Motorcycle Club. In 1954 Otto's new club merged with the Market Street Commandos to become the Hells Angels San Francisco Chapter.

History

The POBOB were one of the earliest motorcycle and car clubs. A few miles south of San Bernardino, California, in the small town of Bloomington in 1945, a particular group of veterans and POBOB founder Otto Friedli who was too young to have served in the war, found civilian life to be too slow and set out to get more thrills by riding motorcycles and hot rod cars. Then on July 4, 1947, in Hollister, California where the American Motorcycle Association (AMA) sanctioned the Gypsy Tour Run, the Boozefighters, POBOB and the Market Street Commandos took over the town for nearly three days. The POBOB members played an integral role in the Hollister riot, on which the movie *The Wild One* was based, starring Marlon Brando.

Two months later, the same clubs went to Riverside, California for the Labor Day weekend, another AMA-sanctioned event. The same thing happened again as it did in Hollister. Over four thousand people, bikers and citizens, took over the town's main street. A Riverside sheriff, Carl Rayburn, blamed a bunch of punk kids for disrupting his town, saying "They're rebels, they're outlaws."

Six months later, Otto Friedli and some disgruntled POBOB members formed the first Hells Angels charter on

March 17, 1948, in San Bernardino, also known as "Berdoo". That same year, the AMA made a statement that ninety-nine percent of the motorcyclists are good people enjoying a clean sport and it's the one percent that are anti-social barbarians. The term "one percenter" is born.

Three years later the P.O.B.O.B. MC came back as a motorcycle club (minus the car club), in the city of Fontana known as Felony Flats. The club still exists today with a group of members known as the **Pissed Off Bastards of Berdoo**, throughout California and Nevada.

Rebels Motorcycle Club

Rebels Motorcycle Club

Motto: "Australia Outlaws Elite" RFFR
Founded: 1969
Location: Brisbane, Queensland, Australia
Founder: Clint Jacks
Leader: Alex Vella
Leader title: National President
Type: Outlaw motorcycle club, non-profit organization
Region: Australia, New Zealand, Germany, Italy, Spain, Fiji
Marque: Harley-Davidson
Membership: 2,000+
Website: www.rebelsmc.net

The **Rebels Motorcycle Club** is an outlaw motorcycle club in Australia with around 70 chapters and 2,000+ members nation-wide making it the largest club in the country. It was founded by Clint Jacks in Brisbane, Queensland in 1969 and was originally named the "Confederates". Their insignia is a Confederate flag with a cap-wearing skull and 1% patch in the centre. The Australian government and law enforcement consider the Rebels to be a criminal organisation but the club claims to be a group of motorcycle enthusiasts rather than gangsters. The National President is currently former boxer Alex Vella.

Its constitution states it is a non profit organization which promotes the riding of Harley-Davidson motorcycles and stipulates that members must own one and that drugs are "looked down on" within club and "something you and your club can go without" with heroin and smoking methamphetamine being totally taboo. Members are only permitted to join the club once and never to join another motorcycle club.

It claims to be "the biggest all big twin Harley-Davidson club in the world", even though many United States members ride Hondas.

Criminal activities

In November 2000, police raided Rebels clubhouses in New South Wales, Queensland and Western Australia and seized drugs, firearms and even a crocodile. A number of people were arrested on charges relating to the items seized.

Two Rebel associates were arrested for the murder of Bandidos member Ross Brand after their clubhouse was raided, on 16 November 2008. Brand was shot dead outside the Bandidos clubhouse in Breakwater, Victoria on 22 October.

A series of raids across Australia ended in 27 members of the Rebels being arrested on a number of charges, on 23 April 2009. Drugs, including methamphetamine, heroin and cocaine, were seized as well as firearms, cash, stolen goods and stolen vehicles.

On 18 May 2009, Michael Paul Falzon was sentenced to ten years in prison for the trafficking of a dangerous drug. He produced methamphetamine (speed) in Mackay, Rockhampton and Dalby and used the Rebels to transport and sell it throughout Queensland and South Australia. The drug ring operated from 1999 until 2003 and made at least $1.5 million.

On April 14, 2012, Anthony "Rooster" Perish (a Gypsy Joker Motorcycle Club member), his brother Andrew (a Rebels Motorcycle Club member) and Matthew Lawton were sentenced to eighteen, nine and fifteen years imprisonment for the homicide of convicted Sydney drug trafficker Terry Falconer, as well as firearms and drug dealing offences

Overseas expansion

In January 2011 the New Zealand Police announced that the Rebels were attempting to set up a New Zealand chapter, and that this was not welcome. New Zealand has reportedly been deporting Australian Rebels members. Despite this, many members wearing rebels patches have been spotted throughout the North Island of New Zealand and it is believed they now have a permanent presence in the country. In Malta the Rebels are very well established, most likely attributable to the close Malta and Australian family connections.

Rebels Motorcycle Club (Canada)

Rebels Motorcycle Club (Canada)

Founded: 1968
Founding location: Red Deer, Alberta, Canada
Years active: 1968-2004
Territory: Western Canada
Allies: Hells Angels

Rivals: Canadian Airborne Regiment, EPS, RCMP

The **Rebels MC** (motorcycle club) was an outlaw motorcycle club based in Western Canada that was founded in Red Deer in 1968.

Along with the Grim Reapers, the Warlords, and King's Crew, the Rebels became one of the four dominant outlaw motorcycle clubs operating in Alberta prior to 1997. By 1997, when the Grim Reapers became part of the Hells Angels in a patch-over ceremony held in Red Deer, Alberta, and after merging with the Loners of Saskatchewan, the Rebels had become a support club of the Hells Angels with four chapters: Edmonton, Calgary, Moose Jaw, and Saskatoon.

In 1976, the Rebels gained a certain level of notoriety, or respect in some circles, due to their much publicized altercations with the Canadian Airborne Regiment when about 40 members of the Airborne showed up with nunchaku, steel bars, baseball bats, and blackjacks, and ambushed 23 Rebels at the club bar. After a skirmish, the bruised and battered paratroopers retreated and the Rebels went back to their business.

In the 1970s and early 1980s (the golden era in Canada for independent one-percenter clubs), the Rebels were the dominant club in the Edmonton area, while the Reapers were the alpha club in Red Deer and Calgary. In the early eighties, as the Reapers grew more powerful and the Rebels less so, the Rebels were warned by the Reapers not to fly the "Alberta" lower rocker on threat of club warfare, so members of the Rebel's Calgary chapter used "Southern Alberta" for the lower rocker and Edmonton members flew "Northern Alberta". King's Crew, meanwhile, were tolerated in their use of "Calgary" as the lower rocker, while the Saskatchewan Rebels, at that point being the dominant club in that province, flew "Saskatchewan" as their lower rocker. In September 1998, the Saskatoon Rebels were patched over to the Hells Angels and the Apollos of Saskatoon became the primary Hells Angels support club there.

The Edmonton chapter of the Rebels folded in 1997, soon after the arrest of then secretary-treasurer Scott Jamieson. In 2004, Joey "Crazy Horse" Morin, aka Joey Campbell, a former associate of the Edmonton chapter of the Rebels, and Robert Charles Simpson were gunned down outside an Edmonton strip club. At the time of the murders, the Bandidos website identified Morin as a probationary member and Simpson as a hangaround. Sources close to the investigation speculated at the time that Morin and Simpson were in Edmonton to set up shop and the murders were committed by a group opposed to that happening. To date no arrests have been made and the file is still officially open and active.

The Rebels were listed as an *Outlaw Motorcycle Gang* by Criminal Intelligence Service Canada.

Rock Machine

Rock Machine

Founded: 1986
Founding location Montreal, Quebec, Canada
Years active: 1980s–to present
Territory: Throughout Ontario, Quebec & Manitoba Canada, United States, Australia,   Germany, Switzerland, Indonesia
Ethnicity: Mostly French Canadian & Irish Canadian
Membership: 200 members approx. worldwide
Allies: Bandidos, Outlaws Motorcycle Club
Rivals: Hells Angels (1986-2002), Rebels Motorcycle Club (Perth, Western Australia)

Rock Machine, or **The Rock Machine M.C.**, is an outlaw motorcycle club with six Canadian chapters, six US chapters and eight chapters in Australia. It was formed in 1986 by Salvatore Cazzetta, a former friend of Hells Angels Quebec chapter president Maurice Boucher, and competed with the Hells Angels for the street-level drug trade in Montreal. The Quebec Biker war would see Rock Machine form an alliance with a number of other gangs. The conflict occurred between 1994 and 2002 and resulted in over 160 casualties and an unknown number of injuries.

When the Rock Machine became a probationary chapter of the Bandidos motorcycle club in December 2000, after being an official hangaround club for eighteen months, Bandidos national officer Edward Winterhalder was put in charge of overseeing the transition by Bandidos international president George Wegers. The original version of the Rock Machine (1986 - 1999) in Canada changed their colors from black & silver to red & gold in May 1999; their colors remained red & gold until they became Bandidos in December 2000.

After the few remaining Bandidos members in Canada quit the organization and Bandidos Canada was dissolved, ex-members of the Mongols and the Bandidos reformed the Rock Machine in 2007, adopting the original black & silver colors as their patch. As of 2008, the latest incarnation of Rock Machine claims to be a club of motorcycle enthusiasts that is not involved in criminal activity.

Early history

In approximately 1982, Salvatore Cazzetta was a member of the "SS", a white supremacist motorcycle gang based in Pointe-aux-Trembles, on the eastern tip of the Island of

Montreal. Fellow SS member Maurice Boucher became friends with Cazzetta and, as leaders of the gang, the pair became candidates to join the Hells Angels when the gang expanded into Canada.

A Lennoxville, Quebec chapter of the Hells Angels suspected in March 1985 that the Laval chapter was interfering with drug profits through personal use of products intended for sale. It is believed that the Laval chapter's invitation to a Lennoxville chapter party led to the ambush and death of five Laval members. Divers located the decomposing bodies of the victims at the bottom of the St. Lawrence River, wrapped in sleeping bags and tied to weightlifting plates, two months after the party. The event became known as the Lennoxville massacre, and its extreme nature earned the Quebec chapter of the Hells Angels a notorious reputation. Cazzetta considered the event an unforgivable breach of the outlaw code and, rather than joining the Hells Angels, in 1986 formed his own smaller gang, the Rock Machine, with his brother Giovanni.

Future Rock Machine leader Fred Faucher later stated, "Sal once told me, "Those guys [Hells Angels], they operate their club in such a way that I didn't want to join them"". Rock Machine members chose not to wear Hell's Angels-style leather vests that could easily identify members, but instead wore rings displaying an eagle insignia. The official Rock Machine club motto is "A La Vie A La Mort", or "In the life and death".

Boucher, after finishing a forty-month sentence for armed sexual assault, joined the Hells Angels and was subsequently promoted within the club's ranks. The Hells Angels and Rock Machine co-existed peacefully for many years, a situation that, according to police officials, was due to Boucher's respect for Cazzetta and the latter's connections with the Quebec Mafia, the only organized crime group that the motorcycle gangs were unwilling to attack.

Quebec Biker war

Main article: Quebec Biker war

Cazzetta was arrested at a pitbull farm in 1994 for attempting to import eleven tons of cocaine. Recently promoted Hells Montreal president Boucher began to increase pressure on the Rock Machine shortly after the arrest, which initiated the Quebec Biker war. The much smaller gang Rock Machine formed an affiliation, "the Alliance", with Montreal crime families such as the Pelletier clan and other independent dealers who wished to resist the Hells' attempts to establish a monopoly on street-level drug trade in the city. A violent turf war ensued with the Hells Angels.

Boucher organized "puppet clubs" to persuade Rock Machine-controlled bars and their resident drug dealers to surrender their illegal drug business. Rock Machine resistance led to bloodshed. Two members of the Hells Angels' top puppet club entered a downtown motorcycle shop on July 14, 1994, and shot down a Rock Machine associate. "That was the beginning of the war," Ouellette said.

A Jeep wired with a remote-controlled bomb exploded that August, killing a Rock Machine associate and an 11-year-old boy, Daniel Desrochers, who was playing in a nearby schoolyard. The first full Hells Angels member was shot to death entering his car at a shopping mall a month later.

Nine bombs went off around the province during his funeral."

This turf war prompted the Rock Machine to align itself with the Bandidos motorcycle club from Texas.

Ten individuals allegedly displaying Rock Machine colours were spotted on July 21, 2011, in a downtown Montreal strip club, the location where a Rock Machine leader had been savagely beaten 10 years previously by Hells Angels associates.

Break from Bandidos

After the 2006 massacre that would claim the lives of eight prominent Bandidos members at a farm house in Shedden, Ontario, the Bandidos Canada closed its doors officially in October 2007. Infighting, lack of support from US and European Bandidos, and the Canadian members' suspicions about their US counterparts' involvement in the Shedden murders led to its closure.

The Rock Machine was reopened in early April 2008 by several disgruntled members of the now-defunct Bandidos Canada "No Surrender Crew", who reorganized it as the Rock Machine Canada Nomads. The move was intended as an insult towards the Bandidos US national chapter and Bandidos National President Jeffrey Pike in particular, but gained unexpected momentum. The club spread across Canada and over several countries including the United States and Australia.

The newly reformed Rock Machine maintains an enmity towards the Texas-based Bandidos national chapter, despite claims in Alex Caine's book *The Fat Mexican*, which state that Rock Machine members in 2008 made a secret deal with high-ranking members of the Bandidos national chapter to re-open in Canada. The club says that it now dismisses members who are involved in any known crimes or criminal activity.

Members

Well-known former members of the Rock Machine included Peter Paradis, who later testified for the Crown at the trials of other members, Richard "Bam-Bam" Lagacé (deceased), Johnny Plescio (deceased), Tony Plescio (deceased), Renaud Jomphe (deceased), Frederic Faucher, Alain Brunette, Bruce Doran, who was instrumental in establishing the Kingston, Ontario chapter, and Paul Porter, who later joined Hells Angels.

The Rock Machine was absorbed into the Bandidos motorcycle club in 2000, in a patch-over ceremony overseen by high-ranking Bandidos member Edward Winterhalder. They would remain Bandidos for 7 years. Many Rock Machine members at the time joined their former archenemy, the Hells Angels, due to the Bandidos' refusal to grant full status to junior-patched members of the Rock Machine.

High-profile members who defected to the Angels included Paul Porter, Nelson Fernandes and Bruce Doran, who joined the Nomads chapter of the Quebec Hells Angels. Fernandes died of cancer within months of becoming a Hells Angel. Doran turned in his colours and returned to private life, but some members of the law enforcement community believe he is still very active and merely uses his resignation as a cover to continue his involvement without the scrutiny of police.

Perth, Western Australia

A Rock Machine chapter was established in the Perth suburb of Myaree, Western Australia in 2009. The defection of a Rebels MC member to the Rock Machine sparked an ongoing violent feud between the gangs in Perth.

The club received negative publicity when Rock Machine associate Stefan Pahia Schmidt was charged with murder after throwing a pub patron through a window with a 7 metre fall. It is alleged that Schmidt was present with other Rock Machine members when the victim spoke with two women from the Rock Machine group.

Road Knights

Road Knights Motorcycle Club

Founded: 1979
Territory: Invercargill, Dunedin, Timaru

The **Road Knights Motorcycle Club** is an outlaw motorcycle club that operates in the South Island of New Zealand with a presence in Invercargill, Dunedin, and Timaru.

Its rivalry with the Mongrel Mob boiled over in June 2008 in Invercargill when the Road Knights' building was burned down and two motorcycles stolen. The motorcycles were later found by police at the local Mongrel Mob headquarters but had been set on fire. Two Mongrel Mob members were charged with the arson.

As of 2009, Road Knights membership in New Zealand was low and former leadership had dispersed, died or gone to jail.

History

The Road Knights Motorcycle Club was founded in 1979.

In the late 1980s, the Road Knights entered into a war with the Damned which resulted in several violent incidents. The first death occurred in October 1987 when Robert Holvey, a Damned associate, was killed with an axle after a ramming incident outside the Invercargill prison. Three Road Knights members were charged with murder, but the charges were later dismissed.

In January 1988, while many police officers were in Arrowtown investigating the murder of Maureen McKinnel, there was a bomb attack against a Waikiwi bank. This was a diversion for a bombing attack against the Road Knights HQ, which caused only minor damage as some of the gelignite bombs failed to detonate. A gang sniper was believed to have been posted to cover the bombers, and shots were fired at a police car. No one was convicted relating to these incidents.

In 2004, Jarrod Mangels was convicted of the 1987 murderer of Maureen McKinnel, which happened before he joined the club.

Satudarah

Satudarah MC

Founded: 1990
Founding location: Moordrecht, Netherlands
Years active: 1990-present
Territory: Netherlands, Belgium, Germany, Spain, Denmark. Sweden.
Ethnicity: Maluku, Dutch, Manush, Surinamese, Dutch Antillean, Moroccan and Turkish
Membership: Around 2000 Worldwide
Allies: Bandidos
Rivals: Hells Angels

Support your local

Satudarah MC is a one-percenter motorcycle club and an alleged organized crime syndicate that was founded in Moordrecht in the Netherlands in 1990. Satudarah MC has 44 chapters throughout the Netherlands and recently opened up new chapters in Belgium, Spain, Indonesia, Malaysia, Denmark, Sweden and Germany. Satudarah MC differs from most other outlaw motorcycle gangs in the fact that it welcomes all races into its club. The ethnic makeup of the club is primarily Ambonese and Dutch, but recently more and more members from Surinamese, Dutch Antillean, Moroccan and Turkish origins have joined its ranks.

Criminal activities

Members of Satudarah MC are frequently brought into connection with drug trafficking, murder, extortion and weapon trafficking. Satudarah MC is being thought of as extremely violent and ruthless, more so than the Hells Angels in the Netherlands. Satudarah MC maintains a close relation with the Bandidos Motorcycle Club in Germany (which is primarily composed of ethnic Turks in Germany). The Bandidos are sworn enemies of the Hells Angels. Satudarah MC is bigger than the Hells Angels in the Netherlands and they seek to take over the control of organized crime.

Sin City Deciples

Sin City Deciples

Motto: Death before Dishonor
Founded: 1966
Location: Gary, Indiana
Type: Outlaw motorcycle club
Region: USA and Europe
Membership: 1,200 members
Abbreviation: SCD, 1934 Express

Sin City Deciples [*sic*] is a "one-percenter" outlaw motorcycle club that started in Gary, Indiana in 1966. Though most club members are black, the club is open to all men, regardless of race or color. The club is known for having a large number of street gang members and having extensive contact network with these gangs as well as a high percentage of military veterans. Members ride Harley-Davidson motorcycles. Members pride themselves on the tight knit brotherhood they have developed over years of riding with each other from state to state. With charters that span from coast to coast in the United States and in Europe, they are one of the oldest and largest black outlaw clubs in existence. *Deciples* is a portmanteau of the words *decibels* and *disciples.*

Criminal activities

Ohio

In 2011, a federal grand jury indicted four members of the Sin City Deciples motorcycle club on charges they used counterfeit cashier's checks to buy $175,000 worth of motorcycles, cars, trucks, and stereo equipment. The suspects targeted private sellers found on the internet – primarily Craigslist – then used fake identities and phoney, computer-generated bank checks to buy the vehicles, according to the indictment. The FBI and U.S. Attorney's Office became involved because the scheme stretched from Ohio into Michigan. The suspects are accused of illegally buying 25 vehicles and two stereo systems, which they either resold whole or disassembled and sold for parts, the indictment said. Several of the vehicles were recovered at the gang's former clubhouse.[2]

In 2013, Dayton Police responded to a disturbance early Sunday morning at the Toro's Motorcycle Club, 1536 W. Third St., where they found a man who was bleeding heavily from the head after being attacked with a machete. The victim, a 33-year-old male, said a large group of men who were members of the Sin City Deciples motorcycle club from Cincinnati had attacked him after one of them bumped into him and they exchanged words.

Pennsylvania

In June 2013, the clubhouse in Pittsburgh was damaged in a suspected arson attack.

Colorado

In 2012, six members of the Sin City Deciples and Sin City Titans were arrested on charges from first degree murder to suspicion of accessory to first-degree murder. On March 3, Virgil Means went to the Sin City clubhouse, known for its wild post-closing hour parties that frequently rage until dawn. Means was forcibly ejected from the club by members and beaten up outside before he was picked up by a friend, according to police testimony in the case. Means and the friend, Mark Nadeau, later drove back to the club to retrieve Means' wallet. While Means sat in Nadeau's stopped Cadillac debating whether or not to get his wallet, three gunmen appeared and opened fired on the vehicle according to testimony.

Indiana

In July 1968, two members of the Gary, Indiana charter of Sin City Deciples were arrested on racially biased charges of assaulting a white woman. This led the remaining club members to start a city wide riot that resulted in fire bombings, sniper fire and wide spread looting. Six persons were reported injured, including a fireman who was shot by sniper fire. It took over a 180 State and local law enforcement agencies to quell the riot, in all 123 persons were charged with resisting arrest and 43 more arrested for breaking curfew.

In June 2011, a wild shootout occurred as the Sin City Deciples' annual cabaret concluded early Sunday left five people wounded one critically, police said. Police recovered dozens of shell casings from at least four different-sized bullets.

Alabama

In 2009, a jury found club member Charlie Joe Wilson, Jr. guilty in the January 11, 2009 execution-style shooting murder of Charles Bevelle in Birmingham on Interstate 20.

Georgia

In 2009, three members on their way to the Annual National Biker's Roundup were arrested on felony charges of theft by receiving a stolen firearm, speeding, possession of marijuana and possession of a firearm by a convicted felon.

Popular media

The Los Angeles chapter of Sin City Deciples was featured in the 2006 movie *Crank*.

Solo Angeles

Solo Angeles CM

Founded: 1959
Location: Tijuana, Mexico
Type: Outlaw motorcycle club
Region: Mexico
Website: www.soloangelescm.com

The **Solo Angeles Club de Motocicletas** (English: Solo Angels Motorcycle Club) is a motorcycle club that was formed in Tijuana, Mexico in 1959. The club's insignia is simply a chopper-style motorcycle. The club does an annual charity run where they deliver toys to poor children in Tijuana.

Razatoy – The Solo Angeles Tijuana toy run

Sons of Satan MC

Sons of Satan Motorcycle Club, known locally as **The Sons**, is an outlaw motorcycle club and support club for the Pagan's Motorcycle Club. It was formed in 1949 and incorporated in 1954 in Lancaster, Pennsylvania by returning World War II veterans. The club was eventually taken over by its namesake, John 'Satan' Marron, who later became the National President of the Pagan's Motorcycle Club. Marron is thought to be the one that converted The Sons from a fairly friendly, family-oriented club into a violent outlaw motorcycle gang. Although The Sons are still a Pagan support club, the club's members have calmed considerably in recent years, apparently returning to their original roots as a quasi-family-friendly club.

History

The Sons of Satan were originally the dominant motorcycle club in Central Pennsylvania, with over 100 members from Lancaster County and surrounding areas. During the 1960s, The Pagans began moving north into Central Pennsylvania which sparked a brief conflict between the two clubs. The conflict was resolved when Sons of Satan President John Marron and Pagans' President Fred 'Dutch' Burhans formally met and became close friends. Marron and a few select Sons members soon moved over to the Pagans while the remaining Sons were allowed to continue their club under Pagan oversight. Marron was later imprisoned after being convicted of maiming and homicide charges in the mid 1970s.

On December 13, 2002, the Sons of Satan clubhouse was destroyed by a pipe bomb explosion while the building was unattended. Although authorities believe it to be the work of rival motorcycle gang, the Hells Angels, the case has yet to be officially solved. After multiple attempts to deny and delay permits by the local zoning commission, the clubhouse was eventually rebuilt.

Sons of Silence

Sons of Silence MC

Motto: donec mors non separat "Until Death Separates Us."
Founded: 1966
Key people: Bruce "The Dude" Richardson
Type: Outlaw motorcycle club
Region: Midwestern and Southern United States; Southern Germany
Membership: 250-275 full-patch members
Website: www.sonsofsilence.com

Sons of Silence Motorcycle Club (SOSMC) is a one-percenter motorcycle club that was founded in Niwot, Colorado in the United States in 1966. The first chapter outside of Colorado was the Iowa chapter which was founded in 1968. There are now American chapters in Arkansas, Florida, Illinois, Indiana, Kansas, Kentucky, Louisiana, Minnesota, Mississippi, Missouri, North Dakota, South Dakota, Tennessee, Utah and Wyoming. The first foreign chapter was founded in Munich, Germany in 1998. In 2001, more German chapters were founded in Freising,

Gangkofen and Nürnberg. In November 2007, a Viernheim chapter was founded.

The Sons of Silence's logo is an American Eagle superimposed over the letter "A" (similar to, and taken from, the Anheuser-Busch logo) flying under an arch and their motto is "*donec mors non separat* ", Latin for "*until death separates us*". The logo is embroidered onto the back of all members' jackets or vests.

Criminal activities

On October 9, 1999, 37 Sons of Silence members were arrested on drug trafficking and illegal weapons charges after one of Denver's largest federal undercover operations. The Bureau of Alcohol, Tobacco and Firearms raided a number of homes and properties in Colorado Springs and Fort Collins, and seized 20 pounds of methamphetamine, 35 guns, four hand grenades, two suppressors, cash and motorcycles. The investigation began in 1997 and involved two undercover agents infiltrating the club. The club was featured in a 2009 episode of *Gangland*, which included interviews with one of the undercover agents who infiltrated the club.

Six Sons of Silence were arrested by the ATF on April 4, 2001 on the charges of trafficking cocaine, cannabis and methamphetamine, as well as firearms, throughout the state of Iowa.

Vagos Motorcycle Club

Vagos MC

Motto: We Give What We Get
Founded: 1965
Type: Outlaw motorcycle club
Region: Southwestern United States and Northern Mexico and Canada and Australia and Europe
Membership: 600 full-patch members
Website: www.vagosmcworld.com
Abbreviation: 22, Green Nation

The **Vagos Motorcycle Club**, also known as the **Green Nation**, is a one percenter motorcycle gang that formed in 1965 in the unincorporated community of San Bernardino, California. The club originally was called "the Psychos".

The club's insignia is Loki, the Norse god of mischief, riding a motorcycle. Members typically wear green.

The Federal Bureau of Investigation as well as the Bureau of Alcohol, Tobacco, Firearms and Explosives and the California Attorney General have named the Vagos as an outlaw motorcycle club, claiming that they are involved in criminal activities such as producing, transporting and distributing methamphetamine and marijuana, as well as assault, extortion, insurance fraud, money laundering, murder, vehicle theft, witness intimidation and weapons violations. The Vagos have approximately 4,000 members among 47 chapters located in the states of Arizona, California, Hawaii, Nevada, Oregon, Utah, Missouri, Several Canadian chapters Peterborough, Ontario,Chapters throughout Europe and ten chapters located in Mexico (Baja California, Jalisco and Mexico City). Two hundred members are in Inland Empire (California), where the club was started in the late 1960s.

In 2013, the Vagos expanded to Sweden and Australia.

In 2002, members of the Vagos turned in the estranged wife of a Pomona, California police detective after she attempted to hire a hit man from the Vagos to kill her husband.

History

During World War II, many military service men rode motorcycles and grew attached to them, and could not leave them after the war. The motorcycle enthusiasts formed clubs around the time hot rods were in style. In 1948, the Hells Angels formed a motorcycle club; their first chapter was in San Bernardino, California. They shared the streets with another motorcycle club named the Psychos. In 1965, a feud occurred among a few Hispanic members of the Psychos; they left the group and created their own club, which is now known as Vagos MC. Their colors pay homage to their founders' Mexican heritage. The club expanded to the Riverside, California and the California high desert areas, and later to Mexico, and also Europe.

Insignia

A member from the Berdoo chapter (slang for San Bernardino) created a patch while he was in prison. It was Loki, the Norse god of mischief. Vagos is Spanish for "traveling Gypsy", or a streetwise person always up to something. Their denim jackets sport their top rockers with their club name integrated into the middle patch, and bottom rockers with their chapter's region or state, as with "SO. CAL", "California", or "Arizona". The middle patch "depicts a muscle-bound caricature of the Norse god of mischief, Loki, set against a green field". Loki is colored red on top of a bike with his hands holding up their club name. One patch the club wears is the number 22 which stands for the 22nd letter of the alphabet, V, standing for Vagos. They also wear two different patches which are a Loki head (do not confuse Loki Head with Loki on the back, two entirely different patches) and a MF patch they are like badges they wear on the front along with a 22 Patch.The MF patch means Motherfucker it is said they receive it by doing something in defense for the Club, as does the Loki head

Membership

Vagos Membership primarily consists of Caucasian and Hispanic males.

Official Chapters

The Vagos have Chapters all throughout Southern California. They have Chapters in the High Desert (California), Inland Empire (California) which includes both Riverside County, California and San Bernardino County, California where they Started, Los Angeles and San Diego. They also have chapters in the states of Hawaii, Oregon, Nevada, and Utah as well as the country of Mexico, the continent of Europe. and Australia.

Vagos MC criminal allegations and incidents

Members of the Vagos Motorcycle Club have been convicted of involvements in criminal acts, some of them very serious, and regularly face allegations of more.

Hemet Traps

On March 17, 2010, amid allegations that Vagos members had fabricated home-made booby traps to maim and kill police detectives in Hemet, California, police arrested at least 30 Vagos members in a multi-state raid Utah, Nevada, Arizona, and California, involving 400 police officers from 60 law enforcement agencies. The police raided 73 locations in Southern California, seizing weapons and drugs, and discovered a meth lab. The raids were the result of several incidents involving booby traps where the club was implicated as responsible:

- On December 31, 2009, the unmarked headquarters of the Hemet Gang Task Force was filled with natural gas, which had been routed into the building through a hole drilled in the roof. Two task force members had detected the gas and backed away without triggering the explosion. The day before that attack, a Vagos funeral was held at a church next to the office.

- On February 23, 2010, a task force member opened a security gate outside the building, causing a homemade zip gun attached to the gate to fire, nearly hitting his head.
- On March 5, a task force member who had parked an unmarked police car in front of a convenience store in Hemet found a homemade pipe bomb hidden underneath the vehicle.

California and federal authorities announced a $200,000 reward for information on these cases. California Attorney General Jerry Brown called the attempts "urban terrorism."Riverside County District Attorney Rod Pacheco said that Vagos members posed an "extreme threat" to law enforcement officers and were notorious for trying to "infiltrate" public safety agencies, by obtaining sworn or non-sworn positions and working undercover to obstruct and dismantle police investigations.

In March 2011, the club sued Riverside County law enforcement for defamation and damages caused by implicating the group to the attacks on the Hemet police officers. On August 1, Riverside County settled the lawsuit, and cleared the club of any involvement with the attacks on the officers. Meanwhile, they had arrested two men that had no ties to the club. The club's attorney, Joseph Yanny, stated he was pleased with the result: "This was never about money. What was important was that the club clear its name and take this shadow off them."

Nugget Casino Shooting

On September 23, 2011, Vagos members were involved in a shooting at John Ascuaga's Nugget in Sparks, Nevada, where Jeffrey Pettigrew, the president of the San Jose, California chapter of Hells Angels was killed, and Vagos members were wounded. The next day, a Vagos member was wounded at a rally from a drive-by shooting. On September 29, police later arrested Ernesto Manuel Gonzales, a Vagos member, at University of California San Francisco, for killing Pettigrew. On December 7, police announced they arrested Gary Rudnick, the vice-president of the Los Angeles chapter of Vagos, since he had instigated the fight that led to the shooting. Rudnick later pleaded guilty to second degree murder in a bargaining agreement. The trial for the two Vagos members, as well as a Hells Angels member who fired at a crowd, was held on October 29, 2012.

Other incidents

In 1974, four Vagos members were convicted and sentenced to death for murdering University of New Mexico student William Velten. The four, Richard Greer, Ronald Keine, Clarence Smith and Thomas Gladish, spent 17 months on death row, but during the appeals process, Kerry Rodney Lee confessed to the murder.

In October 1998, police arrested more than a dozen Vagos members for kidnapping, drug and weapons crimes, following a two-year undercover investigation. In September 2004, state police arrested 26 members and seized more than $125,000 in cash, drugs and guns. On March 9, 2006, law enforcement conducted "Operation 22 Green", which involved 700 personnel from Bureau of Alcohol, Tobacco, Firearms and Explosives and local police and sheriff's departments. The operation resulted in the arrest of 25 Vagos members and associates for violating firearms and drugs policies. It was "one of the largest coordinated law enforcement probes ever conducted in Southern California". The investigators seized 95 illegal firearms, illegal drugs, $6,000 cash, and two stolen motorcycles. An ATF agent called the group a "ruthless criminal bike gang" that deals in "guns, drugs, and death."

In December 2007, police arrested six Vagos members for "charges of first-degree burglary, second-degree robbery, coercion and second-degree kidnapping" that occurred in August 2007. The victim had announced he was leaving the club, but suffered a beating at the Custom Motorcycle auto shop in Grants Pass, Oregon, and was then taken to his home where he was robbed. In February 2010, the ex-president of the chapter involved was acquitted of all charges relating to robbery assault and kidnapping.

Three Vagos members were arrested on June 9 and 10, 2009, and charged with sexually assaulting a woman in San Jose, California. Police investigators told the *San Jose Mercury News* that the victim met the three men in a nightclub on May 4, 2009, and that they had offered to drive her home, but instead they took her to the Vagos clubhouse on Kings Row where she was beaten and sexually assaulted.

On August 13, 2011 law enforcement authorities reported that the Vagos Motorcycle Club and the Galloping Goose Motorcycle Club were involved in a shootout which shut down traffic on I-44 near Lebanon, Missouri. The local 911 Center received about 20 calls, which reported that approximately 20 men were fighting, and that shots had been fired.

Warlocks Motorcycle Club (Pennsylvania)

Founded: 1967
Location: Philadelphia, Pennsylvania
Type: Outlaw motorcycle club
Region: East Coast

The **Warlocks Motorcycle Club** in Pennsylvania is a "one-percenter" Outlaw motorcycle club that was formed in Philadelphia, Pennsylvania in 1967. It was the first official outlaw motorcycle club founded in Pennsylvania. The club is most prominent in the Philadelphia metropolitan area and throughout the Delaware Valley, including Wilmington, Chester, and South Jersey. However, there are now chapters all throughout Pennsylvania, New Jersey, and Delaware. They bear "colors" that are unique to the other Warlocks organizations and are the first Warlocks to possess the 1%er diamond patch, worn on their "colors" over their hearts. The club's insignia is a Harpy, female monsters in the form of birds with human faces, Roman mythology, and their colors are red and white. The club expanded rapidly at the end of the Vietnam War when thousands of ex-soldiers returned to the United States, many to Pennsylvania, feeling outcast from society.

Criminal activities

In December 1988, the individuals associated with the Warlocks kidnapped the then Breed chapter president Craig "Coyote" Gudkneckt. After several Warlock members had been jumped in a Bensalem bar, Gudkneckt was taken to the home of a Warlock where he was tied up, beaten and pistol-whipped. Gudkneckt escaped and in violation of underworld codes against speaking to authorities, went straight to the police to report the crime.

On May 6, 1995 Police Sgt. Ippolito "Lee" Gonzalez of Franklin Township, Gloucester County, New Jersey pulled over Warlocks members Robert "Mudman" Simon and Charles Staples on a traffic stop moments after the two had committed a commercial burglary. Simon shot Gonzalez twice, in the head and neck, and Gonzalez died instantly. Simon later said he shot Sergeant Gonzalez because he did not want to return to prison. Simon was quickly apprehended, pled guilty, and was sentenced to death. In 1999, Simon was stomped to death by Ambrose Harris, another death-row inmate, in New Jersey's Trenton State Prison. Harris argued self-defense, and charges were dropped.

In 2006, Tommy Zaroff, born about 1972 (age 41–42), a former President of the Bucks County chapter of the Warlocks was arrested on suspicion of possessing ten pounds of methamphetamine, and was sentenced to at least five years after pleading guilty to charges including distributing a controlled substance, profiting from illegal acts and conspiracy. On February 4, 2009, Daniel "Dirty Dick" McElheney, born about 1944 (age 69–70), was arrested under his alias Richard McElheney, after his home was raided by police. Police seized six rifles, ten handguns and various illegal drugs.

In October 2008, Pennsylvania State Attorney General Tom Corbett alleged that the Warlocks motorcycle club is involved with a methamphetamine manufacturing operation based in Berks County Pennsylvania. The sting was dubbed "Operation Underground". Corbett said the operation manufactured and distributed $9 million worth of methamphetamine throughout southeastern Pennsylvania and possibly (supplied) to members of the Warlocks motorcycle club, which has allegedly been linked to organized crime and drug trafficking. "The Warlocks have been the subject of other investigations, and we will continue to investigate the Warlock-Spadafora meth connection," Corbett said. He added that the investigation is continuing and he expects more arrests. There were no Warlocks arrested or charged at the time of this press release.

Warlocks Motorcycle Club

Warlocks Motorcycle Club

Motto: To find us, you must be good; to catch us, you must be fast; to beat us, you must be kidding.
Founded: 1967
Location: Orlando, Florida
Founder: Tom "Grub" Freeland
Type: 1%er motorcycle club
Region: USA, Canada, Germany, UK
Website: www.warlocksmc.net

The **Warlocks Motorcycle Club** was founded in 1967 in Florida, USA by ex-US naval servicemen serving on the

USS *Shangri-La* aircraft carrier. It is a "One Percenter motorcycle club" with chapters in various parts of the United States, Canada, UK and Germany. Established by Tom "Grub" Freeland, an ex-US Navy sailor, in Orlando, Florida in 1967, its Mother Chapter is still based there. They have over nine chapters in Florida, two in Georgia, seven in South Carolina, five in Virginia, four in West Virginia, one in New York, two in Ohio, one in minnesota, three in England, two in Germany and three in Canada. There are also several Nomads who live and work in states that don't have Warlocks chapters.

The club's insignia is a blazing eagle between a top and bottom rockers, and their patch colors are crimson red, gold and orange. mottos include "Our Business is None of Your Fucking Business" and "*Warlocks forever, forever Warlocks*" ("*W.F.F.W.*").

Criminal activities

The Warlocks were investigated by the Bureau of Alcohol, Tobacco, Firearms and Explosives in 1991, after Steve Martin, an undercover agent, infiltrated the club, and several members were arrested and released. Again, in 2003 the ATF investigated the Warlocks, and convicted several members of drug and weapon charges once more.

Several members and associates were arrested in a small Alberta, Canada town in March 2014 on weapons charges.

The following is an alphabetical list of **notable outlaw motorcycle clubs**, including current, defunct, or historic.

Name	Year founded	Location founded
Bandidos	1966	San Leon, Texas, United States
Blue Angels	1963	Glasgow, Scotland
The Breed	1968	Jersey City, New Jersey, United States
Brother Speed	1969	Boise, Idaho, United States
Chosen Few	1959	Los Angeles, California, United States
Coffin Cheaters	1970	Perth, Western Australia, Australia
Comanchero	1968	Sydney, New South Wales, Australia
Condemned Few	2005	Queens, New York, United States
Devils Diciples	1967	Fontana, California, United States
Diablos	1961	San Bernardino, California, United States
El Forastero Motorcycle Club	1962	Sioux City, Iowa, United States
The Finks	1970s	Adelaide, South Australia, Australia
Free Souls	1968	Eugene, Oregon, United States
Galloping Goose	1942	Los Angeles, California,

Name	Year founded	Location founded
Motorcycle Club		United States
Gremium Motorcycle Club	1972	Mannheim, Germany
Grim Reapers	1958	Alberta, Canada
Gypsy Joker Motorcycle Club	1956	San Francisco, California, United States
Hangmen Motorcycle Club	1960	Richmond, California, United States
Head Hunters	1967	West Auckland, New Zealand
Hells Angels	1948	Fontana, California, United States
Hell's Lovers	1967	Chicago, Illinois, United States
Hessians MC	1968	Costa Mesa, California, United States
Highwaymen	1954	Detroit, Michigan, United States
Invaders	1965	Gary, Indiana, United States
Iron Horsemen	1960's	Cincinnati, Ohio, United States
Jus Brothers	1990	San Joaquin County, California, United States
Lone Legion	?	Blenheim, New Zealand
Lost Breed	1976	Nelson, New Zealand
Market Street Commandos	1940s	San Francisco, California, United States

Name	Year founded	Location founded
Mobshitters	1970	Hurtsville, New South Wales, Australia
Mongols	1969	Montebello, California, United States
Notorious	2007	Sydney, New South Wales, Australia
Outlaws	1935	McCook, Illinois, United States
Pagan's	1959	Prince George's County, Maryland, United States
Peckerwoods MC	1978	Santee, California, United States
Pissed Off Bastards of Bloomington	1945	Bloomington, California, United States
Phantom Motorcycle Club	1968	Chicago, Illinois, United States
Rebels Motorcycle Club	1969	Brisbane, Queensland, Australia
Rebels Motorcycle Club	1968	Red Deer, Alberta, Canada
Red Devils	c. 1940	Hamilton, Ontario, Canada
Rock Machine	1980s	Montreal, Quebec, Canada
Road Knights	1979	Timaru, New Zealand
Satan's Sidekicks		Detroit, Michigan, United States
Satan's Soldiers	1980	Bronx, New York, New Jersey, United States.

Name	Year founded	Location founded
		Australia
Satudarah	1990	Moordrecht, Netherlands
Sin City Deciples	1966	Gary, Indiana, United States
Solo Angeles	1959	Tijuana, Mexico
Sons of Satan MC	1954	Lancaster, Pennsylvania, United States
Sons of Silence	1966	Niwot, Colorado, United States
Vagos	1965	Temescal Valley, California, United States
Warlocks	1967	Philadelphia, Pennsylvania, United States
Warlocks	1967	Orlando, Florida, United States
Wheels of Soul	1967	Philadelphia, Pennsylvania, United States

*"Family reunions are great when
Granny licks my balls."*